Live at the Commodore

LIVE *at the* COMMODORE

THE STORY OF VANCOUVER'S HISTORIC COMMODORE BALLROOM

AARON CHAPMAN

ARSENAL PULP PRESS ✦ VANCOUVER

ARSENAL PULP PRESS
Suite 202–211 East Georgia St.
Vancouver, BC V6A 1Z6
Canada
arsenalpulp.com

The publisher gratefully acknowledges the support of the Canada Council for the Arts and the British Columbia Arts Council for its publishing program, and the Government of Canada (through the Canada Book Fund) and the Government of British Columbia (through the Book Publishing Tax Credit Program) for its publishing activities.

The Commodore Ballroom's name and likeness is used with the permission of Live Nation Canada, Inc.

Efforts have been made to locate copyright holders of source material wherever possible. The publisher welcomes correspondence from any copyright holders of material used in this book who have not been contacted.

Photographs used in this book remain the property of copyright holders listed in the captions.

Editing by Susan Safyan
Book design by Gerilee McBride
Proofreading by Linda Field and Kerrie Waddington
Back cover photos; (top) City of Vancouver Archives CVA 780-51; (bottom) 1999 Renovation floor plan, Courtesy Neptoon Records Archives

Printed and bound in Canada

Library and Archives Canada Cataloguing in Publication

Chapman, Aaron, 1971–, author
        Live at the Commodore : the story of Vancouver's historic Commodore Ballroom / Aaron Chapman.

Includes index.
Issued in print and electronic formats.
ISBN 978-1-55152-566-2 (pbk.).—ISBN 978-1-55152-567-9 (epub)

        1. Commodore Ballroom. 2. Music-halls—British Columbia—Vancouver.
3. Rock music—British Columbia—Vancouver—History and criticism. I. Title.

ML3534.6.C2C466 2014   781.6609711'33   C2014-906491-8
                                                       C2014-906492-6

CONTENTS

{ Granville Street, 2013.
Photo: Milos Tosic }

One

ONCE UPON A SATURDAY NIGHT

It's Saturday night on Granville Street. While Granville stretches nearly six miles (ten km) down the middle of Vancouver, it's the five-block strip between Drake and Robson Street that encompasses the city's nightclub district. Granville Street is looking better now than it used to; gone is much of the rough and tumble atmosphere, and the daytime drunks and other down-and-outers, common sights as recently as the 1990s, have died off. Many of the old stores, family businesses, and woebegone pawn shops, once seemingly permanent fixtures of the downtown south end of the street, have also disappeared, along with some of the theatres and nightclubs that made this section of Granville the city's entertainment strip for more than eighty years.

At the corner of Drake Street, you'll still see the venerable Yale Hotel, but you won't hear twelve-bar blues there any more. After more than twenty-five years as a regular stop for a who's who of travelling blues musicians—including Pinetop Perkins, Clarence "Gatemouth" Brown, and many local artists—the legendary blues nightspot closed in 2011 after neighbouring condominium construction and hotel renovations

Granville Street, 2013. Photo: Milos Tosic

shuttered the business. Heading on, you pass the Morrissey Pub, once the home of the Austin Flash One strip club—just one of the many strip bars that thrived downtown until the mid-1990s. At Davie Street you'll see a couple of the area's ubiquitous pizza-by-the-slice shops, which keep themselves busy with nightclub patrons headed up to the gay clubs on Davie or further down Granville to the new clubs there.

Past Davie, and past the old Cruel Elephant nightclub that was home to local and touring punk rock bands in the early 1990s before it relocated to Vancouver's Gastown district and eventually disappeared, is a Wings restaurant that proudly advertises twenty-one kinds of chicken wings. On the other side of the street, in the St. Helen's Hotel, was once the Buffalo Club, a rock 'n' roll room in the early 2000s, now the Cabana Lounge, whose atmosphere emulates the South Beach chic of Miami, where everyone thinks they're a VIP.

Mac's Leathers, with its vivid window displays of mannequins in gay bondage gear, is gone, but one Granville Street sex shop remains, a throwback to the early '80s; they are open twenty-four hours a day, selling adult magazines and toys. But even this part of the street is undergoing gentrification.

The old Sugar Refinery was an intimate live music room for local experimental folk and jazz groups, which had the atmosphere of an old coffee house; it's also gone, now replaced by an "urban wine lounge." There's no show to watch there tonight. Where its small stage was once located, there's just a DJ, her face aglow as she sits staring closely at her Mac laptop.

Past FanClub, a newer bar with some promise run by the Yale's former owners, the single room occupancy hotels that once housed derelict old men are now full of young men with

Australian and Irish accents. The sleazy hotels have been renovated into clean Backpackers Hostels with racks of tourist brochures and visitor information for young travellers overstaying their summer visas.

At Doolin's Irish Pub on the corner of Nelson, none of tonight's patrons remember when a very young Michael Bublé sang there (when it was known as BaBalu's in the late 1990s), or knows that David Lee Roth once booked the entire top floor of the Nelson Hotel when he and his entourage were in Vancouver to record an album, but spent most of their time at Champagne Charlie's, the strip bar in the hotel's dingy basement that had a lot more to do with charlie than with champagne.

The Penthouse Nightclub is still a busy spot, around the corner on Seymour Street, where it's been since the 1940s, but the streets themselves are tamer now. It wasn't the police but rather the new condominium developments that finally pushed the street workers, female and male, out of the neighbourhood. You can't beat a condo strata committee; they always win in the end.

At Nelson Street, on the 900 block of Granville, Vancouver's "Entertainment District" really begins, and is where the first signs that Theatre Row—an old term for this part of Granville—has all but disappeared. Generations of Vancouverites once came to stroll beneath the neon and marquee lights of the half-dozen old movie theatres that once lined this stretch of Granville Street; almost all of these theatres have now been gutted and turned into new nightclubs.

On Friday and Saturday nights, the police cordon off this section of Granville to provide better police and ambulance access and to allow pedestrian traffic to spill into the street itself; the police have found that crowds with more room fight less. Tonight, the lights of a cop car are flashing at the curb, and officers walk the beat in twos and threes. A group of drunken girls in their early twenties drag a glassy-eyed friend who stumbles in her high heels like a foal just learning to take its first awkward steps. A tanned panhandler in tattered jeans repeatedly asks passersby for change, muttering to himself as he accosts a group of young men headed to the Roxy, the Republic, the Caprice, the Granville Room, Furniture Warehouse, Joe's Apartment, the Speakeasy, the Cinema Public House, or one of the many other bars in the 900 block.

Not all is lost or changed since the glory days of Theatre Row, however. The Vogue Theatre, with its refurbished neon sign, one of the brightest on the street, is still standing, and inside, much of its 1940s-era décor has been preserved. For some years, its stage was underused and it seemed doomed to be remodelled into a high-end supper club. Now the Vogue is a successful live-concert venue that hosts high-profile touring acts. In its shadow, the little Movieland Arcade is also still there, like a fossil caught in amber, with rows of blinking stand-up video-game cabinets that must seem laughably rudimentary to today's Xbox generation. Here, the last vestiges of Theatre Row are holding out in the coin-op, 8mm "girlie movies" for men who sit in tiny booths with sticky floors. It's now the only place on Granville where you can see a movie.

Things seem to shift at the 800 block, and the nocturnal hum of Granville changes too. Young crowds still head south to the bars, but a different atmosphere takes over, and it's not just because of the grey-haired audience leaving the Orpheum

Granville Street, 2013. Photo: Milos Tosic

Theatre after a Vancouver Symphony Orchestra concert, the one occasion these days when a mix of ages is seen on Granville. A little farther north, a lineup is moving its way into a building, and the mood of this crowd suggests that a night of drinking is not the sole reason they're here. With tickets in hand, they're lined up to see a show at the Commodore. There are no police out front—none seem required—and the doormen don't stand with arms folded like goons.

The Commodore Ballroom is regularly voted the best live-music room in Vancouver in local entertainment weekly readers' polls, and it frequently garners mention in national music trade papers as one of the best concert venues in Canada. In 2011, *Billboard* magazine ranked the venue one of the top ten most influential in North America, along with such legendary concert halls as the Fillmore in San Francisco and the Bowery Ballroom in New York. Of all the clubs that made that list, the Commodore is the oldest. Tonight, patrons walk up the venue's broad and elegant staircase, which thousands of people have climbed since the club opened more than eighty years ago.

The best concerts are not necessarily witnessed in enormous stadiums. On any given evening, the greatest show in the world might be happening at the corner dive where the band plays to a handful of people. But the Commodore has seen more legendary concerts than most places, and it could even be argued that the room itself has added to the quality of these performances. That's one of the reasons that the Commodore has endeared itself to the city's music fans, to the staff who've worked there over the decades, and to musicians from around the world who've played there.

Once inside the doors, the crowd winds up the carpeted staircase to a space that has witnessed the history of entertainment itself in Vancouver, and to a renowned dance floor that has seen everything from the Fox Trot and Jitterbug to slam-dancing and moshing. The history of the room is the history of how Vancouver has entertained itself, almost from its beginning.

The Broadway Café at 105 East Hastings Street was
owned by Nick Kogos, who opened the Commodore
Café in 1924. Photo: Philip Timms, 1922, in
Vancouver Public Library, Special Collections, 7462

THE TWENTIES ROAR

Two

BECAUSE IT WASN'T established until the last quarter of the nineteenth century, the city of Vancouver was shaped by the twentieth century. It's difficult now to appreciate just how different Vancouver was in the 1920s and early 1930s from the city we know today, and just how unlikely it was that the Commodore was built at such a turbulent time in the young city's history.

In the 1920s, upheavals like World War I and the 1918 Spanish flu epidemic were still fresh in people's minds, and day-to-day life was changing significantly. While born-and-bred Vancouverites of the 1920s grew up isolated from the rest of the world, their children were increasingly connected by telephone and radio, and their lives modernized by conveniences such as gas, running water, sewers, and, perhaps most important of all, electricity.

Still, Vancouver itself was a wilder and rougher place than we can imagine today. In the early 1930s, two-thirds of the city streets were still unpaved gravel or dirt, and on its few cobblestone streets, the clip-clop hooves of delivery horses could be heard alongside the growing number of "ah-ooo-gah" car horns. Streetcars operated throughout the city's

neighbourhoods, but the interurban train that transported people to and from the suburbs ran through areas so undeveloped that the lineman at the front of the train cars often carried a rifle to guard passengers from wildlife on the tracks.[1]

Vancouver even smelled different. Although today residents can't burn raked autumn leaves in a backyard fire pit without a permit from city hall, in the 1920s smoke continuously coughed from the mills and industry that surrounded False Creek and the sawdust- and coal-burning furnaces commonly found in most residential homes, dirtying the skies until the inevitable rains—which Vancouverites have always had an ambivalent relationship with—washed the smoke away.

And yet, as small and provincial as it was, the city's future appeared to hold great promise. By 1922, the same year that British Columbians ceased driving on the left side of the road and replaced the Union Jack with the Red Ensign, Vancouver saw a construction boom that, for a while, appeared to have no end. By 1928, work had begun on the Art Deco style Marine Building on Burrard Street that, when complete, would briefly be the tallest building in the British Empire. That same year, work had started just up the street on the new Hotel Vancouver, and outside the city, plans were afoot for the construction of Vancouver Airport on Sea Island.

Vancouverites were also beginning to hear new sounds from far away, carried to them on radio waves. Records show that there were 103 licensed radios in the city in 1922, but in less than a decade, as radios became more affordable and popular, that number would jump to 21,000.[2] The expanding broadcast industry brought sound directly into the homes of people who previously might have heard music only if there were an instrument in the house and a family member who could play it. The relationship people had to music changed; radio gave rise to an interest in popular songs and tunes, and listeners followed the new celebrities of radio dramas in newsstand magazines such as *Radio Times* and *Radio Stars*. While Vancouver listeners could tune into American radio stations, new local stations included CKWX and CJOR.[3]

Some entertainment and nightlife trends of the period sound nearly ancient to modern tastes. For example, in the early 1920s, college debates were the rage in Vancouver. Gatherings known as "smokers" or "smoking concerts" were held in halls, where "for a modest sum, each man was issued a cheap pipe, some tobacco, a bottle of beer, and an apple. There was community singing, solo songs, skits, maybe some witty talks, always an adequate pianist, and maybe some boxing."[4]

In the 1920s and '30s, the focus of the city centre shifted from the harbourside, industrial area of Gastown to the shops, hotels, and businesses of the Granville Street area, as Vancouver became a destination for touring vaudeville acts. By the late 1920s, Vancouver would rival Montreal to the east and San Francisco to the south, where the biggest vaudeville and burlesque stars of the day performed. The city served as a starting point for tours, allowing performers to get a few shows under their belts before they travelled to larger cities in the US.

The three blocks of Granville Street between Nelson and Georgia became an emerging hub of entertainment. The opulent Vancouver Opera House, next to the Hotel Vancouver, had been built for $100,000 in the 1890s and was advertised as the "finest theatre west of the Great Lakes."[5] The Opera House booked the best talent that the European and American stages had to offer and some of the biggest stars of the day, including actors Sir Henry Irving and Sarah Bernhardt, boxer John L. Sullivan, and the Gaiety Burlesque. Yet it was the rise of silent movies that began to make Theatre Row on Granville Street a destination for those looking for something new.

When the Capitol Theatre opened on March 12, 1921, famous silent-film star Wallace Reid, once billed as "the most popular screen idol in America," burst through a paper screen while singing and dancing, to great applause. With a blare of trumpets, the Capitol Theatre Orchestra played an overture, and Mayor R.H. Gale took the stage, stating what a great day it was for Vancouver's progress. Before the "photo-play" began, he told the audience that he hoped the evening would "provide a clean and uplifting picture" for the 2,076 Vancouverites in attendance. They might not have known it yet, but the Roaring Twenties were about to begin on Canada's west coast.

For just fifty cents in the afternoon and seventy-five in the evening, audiences could get a good seat at the Capitol. This was the decade that saw the rise of cinema, when actors such as Charlie Chaplin, Mary Pickford, and Rudolph Valentino became stars. The new gloriously designed Orpheum Theatre opened (at its present location) off Granville and Smithe in 1927 with over 2,800 seats, making it one of the biggest theatres in Canada. The Orpheum stage saw the end of the vaudeville era, and its screen become more significant as the new "talking pictures" were released.

Aside from the first "talkies," there was more to be heard, including the warm reverb of the Wurlitzer organ that often accompanied silent films. This would have been a remarkable time to be a Vancouver musician. Like other theatres downtown, the Capitol hosted vaudeville, theatre, dance contests, and music concerts, where Calvin Winter and his Capitolians orchestra were mainstays. The "jazz age" was in full swing, and between Winter's group and the pit orchestra at the Orpheum, as many as forty musicians worked nightly on that single block of Granville alone.

Thanks to a decade of prosperity, Vancouver saw a new generation earn higher wages as the city expanded, fuelled both by property speculation and increased shipping, which led to the growth of the port. The sawmill and dockyard workers still enjoyed their beer parlours, but those who felt that the saloons and cinemas might be beneath them turned to the elegant atmosphere of the Crystal Ballroom in the old Hotel Vancouver.

Legendary Vancouver bandleader Dal Richards, who turned ninety-six in 2014 and has witnessed much of Vancouver's entertainment history, recalls the ballroom that once stood in the Hotel Vancouver: "It was beautiful and grand. The Crystal Ballroom [was] adjoined by what they called Peacock Alley, which was a broad entrance hall that went down the full length of the ballroom. It had antique furniture, oriental rugs and all that sort of thing, brass railings. Below that, in the lower level, dancing all year was done in what was called the Spanish Grill. That was the nightclub of the hotel, that's where the orchestras played."[6]

Len Chamberlain and His Twinkletoes were the Crystal's house band until Lafe Cassidy's orchestra took over in 1928. It was here that Vancouver's most well-to-do might dine on the most expensive items on the menu—Scalloped Chicken à la King, French Steak Sauté, or Roast Haunch of Spring Lamb

One of the Reifel family businesses was Vancouver Breweries at 11th and Yew streets, shown here in 1926. Although the brewery was demolished in the late 1980s, it was rebuilt and its tower was incorporated into the condominium complex that replaced it. Photo: City of Vancouver Archives, CVA 99-3063

with Mint Sauce. To Vancouver's elite, it must have seemed like the party would never end. In this lavish setting one night in the late 1920s as the orchestra played and couples dressed in their evening finery waltzed on the Crystal's ballroom floor, candles flickering on tables beneath dim lights, the idea for the Commodore was born.

It might be said that the Reifel family, then one of the city's wealthiest, made money the old-fashioned way—by selling alcohol during the US Prohibition and then investing cannily in real estate. Henry Reifel and his brothers Jack and Conrad had emigrated from the Alsace-Lorraine area of Germany in 1886, and after working in breweries throughout California and Oregon, settled in British Columbia and started a single brewery on Vancouver Island. In a few years, they owned four breweries and two distilleries in the Lower Mainland under the name Brewers & Distillers Limited of Vancouver, along with a legal export business.

While exporting liquor from Canada was not illegal, importing it into the United States was, since between 1920 and 1933 the 18th Amendment established Prohibition. The Bronfman family of Montreal became wealthy during this era by bootlegging their Seagram's whiskey; for the Reifels it was not "rum running" that made their fortune, but capitalizing on America's thirst for beer. Shipping it out of Canada was made relatively easy by avoiding the land border crossings, instead sending the cargo by boat. A series of complicated loopholes in the exportation of liquor, which often involved the obscuring of ships' manifests, made such shipments to the US possible. Schooners did a roaring trade leaving Vancouver for falsely documented destinations such as third-party, non-US ports where they failed to unload their cargo, only to clandestinely arrive later at American docks or meet up, while still at sea, with US boats in order to deliver their illicit goods. By the mid-1920s, the Reifels had further profited at home from provincial legislation that had, in effect, given their breweries a monopoly on the business because beer parlours in British Columbia now exclusively stocked their kegs.

With the money flowing in, Henry's sons George and Harry Reifel became involved in the business, and they eventually branched out into what has been Vancouver's all-time favourite industry for those who have money and want more—real estate. George Reifel started Vested Estates Ltd., a real estate and insurance company with an office at 1200 Homer Street. The company would eventually own and rent out dozens of properties between the 800 and 1000 blocks of Granville Street. In early 1929, Vested Estates was still in its infancy, but with the brewery business showing great profits, George and his wife Alma could spend their nights in luxury at the city's finer establishments.

According to legend, it was Alma who felt that the Spanish Grill and Crystal Ballroom were getting too crowded and that the city needed another ballroom. One can only wonder what, exactly, Alma said to her husband on that fateful night, but she planted the seed in George's mind. Was George tantalized by the prospect that he could call a place like the Crystal his own? Luckily, he had the wealth to make these grandiose dreams a reality.

George Reifel selected Vancouver architect Henry Herbert Gillingham to design the ballroom. Gillingham had been born in London, England, in 1876. He arrived in Vancouver during a housing boom in 1911 and went on to design various commercial buildings and a grand home in Vancouver's upscale Shaughnessy neighbourhood. In *Building the West: The Early Architects of British Columbia*, Donald Luxton notes that "Gillingham's house designs show a distinctive British arts and crafts sensibility."[7] Reifel's new venue was to be modelled after the classic English ballrooms of the period, but in the contemporary Art Deco style.

Reifel and Gillingham envisioned a whole complex, with a basement bowling alley and billiards area, ground-floor retail space, and a new ballroom cabaret on the second floor. It was just a matter of finding the space in which to build. If the new ballroom was to serve the patrons of the Hotel Vancouver, it needed to be close by. Granville Street, with the Orpheum and other theatres now established, was already becoming an entertainment strip.

Reifel found a small two-storey row of storefronts in the 800 block of Granville Street between the Capitol Theatre entrance and the Norfolk Rooms Hotel and next door to the Orpheum Theatre. The stores were a mix of small businesses, including a menswear shop, bakery, pork sausage manufacturer, radio store, dance academy school with second-floor space that sold Japanese goods, and a small nightspot called the Commodore Café, run by Nick Kogos (whose name has been spelled both Kogos and Kogas) and Johnny Dillias.

While Reifel had expertise in the brewery and real estate businesses, he likely knew little of the entertainment industry, and he needed people with experience to manage the day-to-day aspects of the enterprise. Perhaps since the days of the first village taverns, it's taken a special kind of person to run a bar.

A combination of skills is required, from closely following the rules while cutting corners, to being gregarious and friendly with the public yet knowing when to throw someone out, to keeping the police at a friendly distance. It's an occupation that doesn't attract stuffed shirts; Nick Kogos and Johnny Dillias had what it took. Dillias had started out as a waiter at Vancouver's Orpheum Café in 1913. For a time, he worked at Happyland at the Pacific National Exhibition grounds—where he'd gained a reputation for losing more money than he made by giving kids free rides out of his own pocket—but eventually he showed enough business savvy to own the Georgia Oyster Saloon at 715 West Georgia.

Nick Kogos, who had come to Vancouver via New York, was a prominent member of the city's Greek community, with twenty years' experience in the restaurant industry. He'd made a name for himself with the Columbia Grille and Empire Café on Hastings Street, along with the successful Broadway Café at Columbia and Hastings. Kogos, however, also came with some baggage. In May 1921, the Broadway Café had been the subject of a Vancouver police department sting in which its Filipino bandleader, L.C. Fernandez, was arrested for selling seven dollars' worth of cocaine to a police informant by the name of Nosey Wilson. When the story hit the press, Kogos denied knowing about drugs in his establishment, protested that the actions of a sole employee were unjustly tarring his business, and portrayed himself as a victim of bad publicity. Just a few months later, he and two others were named as suspects in an alleged arson of the Golden Gate Café, which had burned down a year earlier.[8] But since the early 1920s, Kogos had run his businesses without scandal, and profitably.

Kogos and Dillias opened the Commodore Café in 1924. It was an intimate spot, with only a gramophone, a small linoleum dance floor, and a few booths with tables, but the place became a popular night spot. Reifel decided that Kogos and Dillias had the nightclub experience necessary to run his new ballroom, and the Commodore Café's popularity might be capitalized upon if the name carried over to the new cabaret.

Kogos and Dillias formed the Commodore Cabaret Ltd. in June 1929. George Reifel bought most of the lots on the block, the old stores were demolished, and work began on the new building. With Reifel's money backing the construction of the grand new building and their own business plans ready, Kogos and Dillias undoubtedly felt confident that they'd be giving the Crystal Ballroom a run for its money. The cash would soon pour in. It must have felt like nothing could stop them.

....

1 Macdonald, Bruce. *Vancouver: A Visual History*. Vancouver: Talonbooks, 1993, 44.

2 Macdonald, *Vancouver*, 40.

3 The Canadian Broadcasting Corporation (CBC) would not have a local station until 1933. MacDonald, *Vancouver*, 44.

4 Davis, Chuck. T*he Vancouver Book: An Urban Encyclopedia*. Vancouver: Evergreen Press, 1976, 414.

5 Davis, *The Vancouver Book*, 412.

6 Mackie, John. "Vancouver's Lost Landmarks," *Vancouver Sun,* April 8, 2011.

7 Luxton, Donald. *Building the West*. (Vancouver: Talonbooks, 2007), 383.

8 "Three Named in Arson Charge," *Vancouver Daily World*, August 15, 1921, 9.

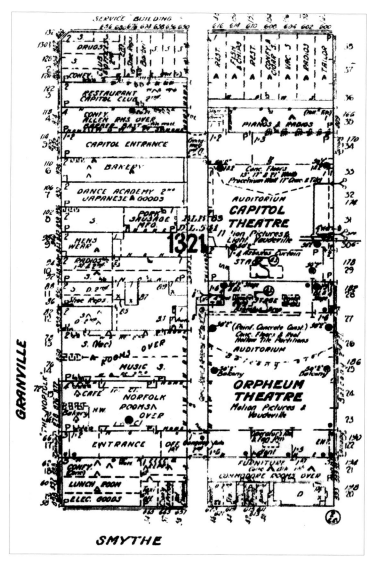

The October 1928 fire insurance map details the 800 block of Granville Street before the Commodore was built. City of Vancouver Archives, CVA Map 599

The COMMODORE CABARET

Opens Wednesday

872 Granville S

VANCOUVER CITIZEN'S LIFE AMBITION REALIZED

It is not often that a life's ambition is so thoroughly realized as it has been by Nick Kogos, one of Vancouver's best known restaurant proprietors, in his conception and construction of the Commodore Cabaret on Granville Street.

Not only has the Commodore a dancing floor that measures 40 feet by 75 feet, but it is equipped with a full stage, carrying the Commodore orchestra of 11 pieces. The lights,

senior, was responsible for many of the city's most beautiful residences.

At the rear of the room, and on each side of the stage, are three rooms that may be used for banquets or private gatherings. These are the Planet room, designed with a view to showing the planets of the sky; the Silver room, all decorated in silver,

The interior decoration is truly the work of experts. The Standard Decorators, who are responsible for the artistic decorations of the cabaret and cafe, are one of the oldest and best known firms in B. C., having been in operation here for twenty-two

Article and advertisements for the Commodore Cabaret's opening night. *Vanouver Sun*, Dec. 2, 1930

Three

BROTHER, CAN YOU SPARE A BALLROOM?

FOR MONTHS AFTER Black Tuesday, many people in Vancouver thought that the Wall Street crash of October 1929 would only affect New York and Chicago stock traders and not them. They were wrong. But it took a few years for the real and devastating consequences to reach Vancouver.

A fortunate few, like the Reifel family, were insulated by their wealth and not affected by the Depression. In fact, by 1932, the Reifels had prospered. That year, George Reifel commissioned an opulent three-level mansion on a large property on Vancouver's Southwest Marine Drive. He called it Casa Mia, and it was built in the Spanish Colonial revival style popular on the West Coast in the 1920s and '30s. At 20,000 square feet, the Reifels' home was bigger than the Commodore Cabaret. Also decorated in the Art Deco style, with expensive wood panelling and glittering chandeliers, it had its own bar, a billiards room, eight bedrooms, both men's and women's washrooms, and its own small ballroom with a stage and sprung dance floor like the Commodore's.[9] It was a remarkable home, though one can't help but think that while many Vancouverites struggled with unemployment and homelessness, the occupants of Casa

Opening day at the Commodore Cabaret, December 3, 1930.
Photo: City of Vancouver Archives CVA 99-3855

Mia went blithely through the Depression, shielded against the poverty and want seen elsewhere in the city. (Perhaps things haven't changed in Vancouver. It's still a long way from Southwest Marine to Hastings Street.) Nevertheless, thanks to the Reifels' great wealth, construction at the Commodore continued unabated during the Depression while other significant building projects in Vancouver were cancelled or put on hold.

Architect Henry Gillingham submitted final plans for the Commodore to the city on January 30, 1930, but would not live to see either the worst of the Depression or the new cabaret. In September of that year, Gillingham, aged fifty-five, suffered a cerebral hemorrhage on a Vancouver streetcar and died. His son Bruce, also an architect, was left to complete his father's work on Granville Street. Of all the building projects Henry had designed, the Commodore is the one for which he is remembered.

Like Vancouver's Lions Gate Bridge, which was built by investments from the Guinness family, the Commodore was made possible by the profits from beer. But had the ballroom been suggested as a project even a year later, it might never have been built. The consequences of the Depression were beginning to unfold in Vancouver by 1930, yet construction work moved so quickly that by July 18, 1930, the city approved the water application, and by September, the Commodore Bowling Lanes and Billiards opened in the building's basement. The first of the retail stores, the Bon Ton Bakery, also opened after a handshake deal with Reifel. Things were moving fast, and there was no looking back now.

Interest in the new building going up on Granville Street

was heightened after Kogos and Dillias placed advertisements in local newspapers on December 2, 1930 to publicize the Commodore's official opening the next evening. It was billed as "Vancouver's Latest Attraction," and "a sumptuous full course supper" was promised to those attending, who were encouraged to make their reservations early and to "come prepared for a real rollicking time."[10] In later years, the opening date of the Commodore would be inaccurately given as 1929, but the correct date was Wednesday, December 3, 1930.

On that day, the front page of the *Vancouver Sun* had a large feature about Nick Kogos, with the headline "Vancouver Citizen's Life Ambition Realized." While he was the main financier and owner of the building, George Reifel had taken a back seat as the man behind the Commodore—and perhaps, as long as the rent kept coming from Kogos and Dillias, Reifel was fine with that arrangement. But on opening night, the doors of the new Commodore Cabaret opened at 8:30 to more than 900 people, including George and Harry Reifel and their wives, members of Vancouver's high society, and city aldermen, all of whom got a chance to see the new cabaret, "the finest of its kind on the Pacific coast." The evening featured the Commodore Orchestra along with the exotic Imanoff Quartette dance troupe, "direct from a sensational tour of the Orient," and Vancouver dance teacher Pauline Olson's "Dancing Sweethearts."[11] The entertainment may have been dazzling, but it was the Cabaret itself that most impressed the patrons that night. The ballroom stage was built as a mid-sized orchestra shell with a spotlight controlled from the stage. In the back were three rooms that could be used for banquets or private gatherings of up to 100 people. In the Planet Room,

An evening at the Commodore in 1930.
Photo: Vancouver Public Library Archives 70488

Pauline Olson was a well-known teacher of dancing in Vancouver who ran a studio at 570 Granville Street in the 1930s. Photo: *Vancouver Sun*

perhaps inspired by the discovery of Pluto in February of that year, the ceiling was painted with planets and stars in the night sky. A second room, decorated entirely in silver, was called, of course, the Silver Room. The largest was the Egyptian Room, designed to showcase all things Egyptian, a popular interest after Howard Carter's discovery of King Tutankhamen's tomb in 1922. Sadly, no photos exist of these old spaces, and years later, they were cleared out and renovated to provide bigger backstage areas, dressing rooms, and production space for touring bands.

The jewel in the Commodore's crown, however, lay under the patrons' feet. Gillingham had designed the dance floor to be forty by eighty feet, in the style of an English ballroom and the dance palaces of the era. But the Commodore's dance floor was also "sprung." That is, it was engineered to absorb shocks and it bounced slightly, even more so when there was a full house dancing on it—an advantage over the ordinary floor at the Crystal Ballroom.

Perhaps Vancouver has always been a little too concerned with how it ranks among the world's bigger or better-known cities, but it's clear that the Commodore Cabaret was viewed as a significant development for the city's status. The day after the official opening, the *Vancouver Sun* heralded the new "night club de luxe that compares favourably with those of any eastern metropolis, and eclipses those in cities to the south when measured up as to size, luxurious and modernistic appointments, dancing space, orchestra, service and entertainment."[12] The cabaret's opening was said to mark "a distinct step in the progress of Vancouver."[13]

Ballroom house orchestra Ole Olsen and his Commodores onstage, January 12, 1933. The band featured Jackie Williamson on drums, and third from left, Charlie Pawlett, who led the band after Olsen retired. Photo: City of Vancouver Archives, CVA 99-4293

The Commodore was open six nights a week throughout December and into the new year, as Kogos and Dillias hoped the dinner-and-dance crowd would flock to the city's new nightspot. But things had changed; it was no longer a good time to open a new business in Vancouver. The "we're-in-the-money" years of the 1920s were over, and Vancouverites began to feel the dire economic effects of the Depression. The construction boom had ended, and unemployment among the province's trade union members rose from five to twenty-four percent within just a couple of years.[14] Building projects already underway ground to a halt; the new Hotel Vancouver, for example, remained in a skeletal condition of bare girders and joists for five years.

By the summer of 1931, camps of unemployed and homeless men, many of them veterans of the Great War, began to form in the city. As author Michael Kluckner notes in *Vancouver: The Way It Was*: "About 250 men lived under the eastern end of the Georgia Viaduct, near the BC Electric Works. They were generally called 'Canned Heaters,' for their alleged habit of straining Sterno or Canned Heat through socks for the alcoholic content. About 400 established themselves in tin and cardboard shacks at the city garbage dump at Prior and Heatley," and food line-ups formed behind the First United Church on Gore Street.[15]

During this time, while the effects of the Dust Bowl ravaged the US, the Canadian prairies were hit with a grasshopper plague and drought. Many walked away from their farms and mortgages and took trains west to Vancouver. New arrivals set up a hobo camp at the eastern edge of the Canadian National Railway yards at the grassy border of Clark Drive. There were no more jobs in Vancouver than anywhere else, but it was better to be homeless in Vancouver's moderate weather than to freeze to death on the prairies. Those who still had jobs saw their wages cut back to the point of mere subsistence, so that even working people had little money for recreation. Within a couple of years, as the tax base was reduced by the loss of industries and defaults on mortgages, Vancouver's neighbouring municipalities of Burnaby and North Vancouver were both forced into receivership.

On Granville Street, the Commodore eliminated its cover charge in an effort to attract customers, hoping that, without the fee, people would at least spend their money on dinner and refreshments. Instead, patrons who came to the club spent no money at all. By the beginning of March 1931, just four months after it had opened, the Commodore closed. *Vancouver Sun* columnist R.D. Bouchette lamented the closure in his "Lend Me Your Ears" column: "This saddens me. It means that Vancouver, this metropolis of the Pacific Coast cannot support even one good-class maison de respectable whoopee." He complained that while the city was full of after-hours speakeasies, they were no longer interesting or pleasant, and he considered it an embarrassment that Vancouver couldn't support a proper establishment. Bouchette continued,

New York may have her innumerable illicit night clubs, Montreal may have access to quite nocturnal parlours of song and dance, and London may sensibly allow scores of wine and wiggle shops. But in Vancouver the amusement seeking public in the late hours must have recourse to places which, entirely apart from their illegality, are dreadfully sordid and dull. I suppose that it would be much better for a great many of the rest of us if we stayed home at nights, listened to the radio and never thought of such places as the Commodore. I have no doubt if we did so we would be a great deal wealthier and a great deal duller. But money is only ninety-five per cent important in life—some of that five per cent remaining should be given to frivolity.[16]

Bouchette blamed Kogos and Dillias for eliminating the cover charge, calling it "a stupid policy" that opened the doors to freeloaders and cheapskates, while "discouraging many other persons who were capable of paying. For these people naturally did not want to patronize the Commodore when the place was open to the relatively impecunious." Bouchette suggested that the Commodore charge $2.50 to keep the business going—and separate the decent patrons from the riff-raff.[17] The Commodore's closure didn't last, however. After regrouping, it reopened on May 23, 1931. Billed as a "long awaited event," the evening featured the "Famous Commodore Orchestra" conducted by Wendell Dorey, a banjo player and bandleader originally from Chicago. The better-class citizens of Vancouver were invited back to "Dine and Dance in the Most Luxurious Cabaret on the Pacific Coast." In an effort to increase business, Kogos and Dillias also opened the Commodore for lunch, reduced the number of nights it was open, and took Bouchette's advice at least partially and charged a $1.00 cover.

It worked. The cover kept out the indigent crowd whom Bouchette had disdained and for a time, the cabaret was once again the playroom of the wealthy and powerful. In April 1932, for example, Vancouver police Chief Constable Charles Edgar Edgett was seen entertaining visiting Winnipeg mayor

Charles Edgar Edgett was chief constable of the Vancouver police department in 1931. Cartoon by Jack Boothe (artist), *Vancouver Daily Province*. Licensed under public domain via Wikimedia Commons http://commons. wikimedia.org/wiki/File:Col_Edgett. jpg#mediaviewer

Colonel Ralph Humphreys Webb at a table with a former governor of New York state.[18] Edgett, who had a year earlier been the warden of the British Columbia Penitentiary, later formed the anti-labour Citizens' League to combat what he saw as Communist agitators forming among the unemployed, and went on to become one of the province's most staunch anti-Communist speakers. Mayor Webb, a conservative politician and fierce opponent of the Winnipeg General Strike in 1919, called the strikers "radical agitators" and urged that all Communists should be "dumped in [Manitoba's] Red River" or deported. The Commodore Cabaret wasn't the place for blue-collar working men or even local labour leaders who wanted to caucus over dinner and cigars.

It was Kogos' and Dillias's decision to rent out the ballroom for company parties, student celebrations, and other events for various social organizations that kept the reopened Commodore alive, and in the process, gave it greater significance to the city. Johnny Dillias became the face of the Commodore as he stood each night at the top of the stairs greeting patrons and making connections. Johnny's wife, Marion, who was the office manager and accountant, later recalled him working hard, dealing with the public and seeking new business. "Johnny remembered all their names and their kids' names, and he could tell you what company had a party here ten years back, or what company was booked for a party six months ahead of time. Company parties were a new thing then, and Johnny went after them."[19] In the years following the Depression, as conditions slowly began to improve in the city, the Commodore would benefit from the new business Johnny Dillias found in hosting company events. Safeway employee parties, Cunningham's

Drugs clerk get-togethers, BC Tel staff Christmas parties and company functions, holiday fundraiser presentations and more, all helped the Commodore to stay in business.

But on Saturday nights, when the cabaret was open to the public for dancing, it became *the* place to go because it was known to have the best dance floor in town. Gladys McLaren, a student at the University of British Columbia in the early 1930s, recalled that a typical evening at the Commodore consisted of dinner—"Chicken à la King with a bun"—and dancing. She remembered standing in the slow-moving lineups that wound up the stairs as people waited to have their coats checked. "It was a chance to spot friends in the lineup and see what they were wearing; long sparkling evening dresses, fur stoles and black three-quarter length coats that showed off the gowns underneath. Men in their tuxedos and tails. All the women wore a corsage."[20] Decades later, the smell of gardenias would remind McLaren of nights at the Commodore.

For many, a night out at the Commodore meant an escape from the drudgery of home or work. The music and lighting were romantic, and compared to most people's homes, the Commodore was glamorous and beautiful. A night on the ballroom floor also offered a chance to hold someone close in a perfectly innocent setting, and dancing in public also allowed cracks to appear in the class system. The dance floor etiquette wherein a dancer could go up to another, tap him on the shoulder with an "Excuse me," and dance with his partner, regardless of who they were, was part of the mannered social setting that allowed different echelons of society to intimately interact. The ballroom provided a rare opportunity for men and women to meet one another.

Local Kiwanis Club members perform a Christmas holiday play, "The Toy Maker's Dream," at the Commodore. Photo: Stuart Thompson, 1935, City of Vancouver Archives, CVA 99-4834

A little gin or whiskey also helped the evening along. The Commodore is remembered as one of the great "bottle clubs" of Vancouver during an era when drinking in public, even in a restaurant or nightclub, was illegal. After British Columbia's four-year period of liquor prohibition during World War I, consumption of liquor outside the home was relegated to beer parlours. These were often dreary places, without music, singing, or entertainment of any kind. They had separate entrances for men and "women with escorts" (to prevent prostitutes from entering on their own) and were often located in or next door to hotels—conveniently situated so that if anyone got too drunk, they could get a room and sleep it off rather than become a public nuisance. But their hours of operation were limited, and the parlours sold nothing stronger than beer by the glass, so that patrons didn't get too carried away. Ballrooms, nightclubs, and restaurants operated without liquor licenses, which forced the public to "brown bag it" and discreetly bring their own alcohol hidden in a jacket or a purse. The Vancouver police department regularly staged "dry squad" raids at various nightspots to see if anybody was committing the crime of drinking at a table with friends. As Vancouver orchestra leader Dal Richards recalls, "Teapots were often available, some even containing tea. If a customer happened to have something in his pocket to pour into a teapot to give the brew a tad more bite, was that the proprietor's fault? And if the police should happen to drop in on behalf of the forces for good in the community, checking to see if anyone was imbibing alcoholic spirits, could they be expected to check every teapot? Of course not."[21]

The Commodore wasn't targeted by the police as often as more notorious places like the Penthouse Nightclub. There, owner Joe Phillipponi had drawers made in the tables, which were covered by long tablecloths, where bottles could be hidden—Phillipponi insisted the drawers were to hide ladies' purses. Where the Penthouse had spotters on the roof who could see police cars roaring down Seymour Street, the Commodore had twenty-one stairs between the door on Granville Street and the second floor. As police entered through the front door, a doorman pressed an alarm bell, which alerted the band, who played a special song announced at the start of the evening to signal the patrons to hide their bottles. ("Roll Out the Barrel" was an inspired choice and a favourite among Vancouver bands on these occasions.) The Commodore kept their pressed white tablecloths nearly floor length, long enough to keep bottles hidden underneath the table and well out of sight. The police knew what was going on but found it an impossible situation to control. Constables regularly frequented the Commodore, yet the police had to be seen enforcing the law. Dry squad raids, however, were mostly used to keep a close eye on more problematic nightspots in the city's East End.

All of these shenanigans became part of a night on the town and an evening at the Commodore. While patrons sneaked in drinks and hid the bottles underneath the tables, the dance floor filled with couples grappling with the waltz, the tango, and each other. How many love affairs began on that floor? "Let's Misbehave," the popular song from 1927 suggested.

The Reifels would not escape the decade without being accused of some misbehaviour themselves. In 1934, Henry and George Reifel were arrested on a visit to Seattle, Washington, and charged with conspiracy to violate the US Tariff Act by importing liquor. Essentially, they were named as smugglers by the US government and faced a civil suit that totalled $17,250,000 in fines, penalties, and evaded duties. Henry and George both posted bail at $100,000 each and returned to Vancouver. But when the Reifels did not attend their subsequent hearing, they forfeited their bonds. With their failure to appear in the US courts, they were indicted on the charges.

The case, however, never went to trial. The Reifels' lawyers managed to get the civil suit dropped in July 1935. But it remained a costly and embarrassing incident, compelling them to pay $500,000 in back taxes and fines to the US government. They were forced to resign as the directors of one of their companies.[22] For years afterward, the closest that the Reifels could get to the US without feeling uncomfortable was visiting the family farm in Ladner, about twenty minutes from the border. The family later donated this land to the Canadian government, and today it operates as the George C. Reifel Migratory Bird Sanctuary.

9 The legendary home still stands today, of keen interest to heritage enthusiasts; it was the star attraction for hundreds who attended the 2014 Vancouver Heritage Foundation home tour.

10 "Let's All Celebrate," *Vancouver Sun*, December 2, 1930, 3.

11 Advertisement. *Vancouver Sun*, December 3, 1930, 18.

12 "New Night Club De Luxe Has Brilliant Opening," *Vancouver Sun*, December 4, 1930.

13 Untitled article. *Vancouver Sun*, December 2, 1930, 1.

14 MacDonald, *Vancouver*, 44.

15 Kluckner, Michael. *Vancouver: The Way It Was*. North Vancouver: Whitecap Books, 1984, 58.

16 Bouchette, R.D. "Whoopee in Vancouver," *Vancouver Sun*, March 23, 1931.

17 Ibid.

18 "Saturday Night at the Commodore," *Vancouver Sun*, April 4, 1932.

19 Kendall, Kay. "21 Steps Lead to Nostalgia," *Vancouver Sun*, October 15, 1973.

20 Quoted in McInnes, Emily. *70 Years of the Commodore Ballroom 1929–1999*. Report prepared for Panther Management, 1999, 7.

21 Richards, Dal, and Jim Taylor. *One More Time!: The Dal Richards Story*. Madeira Park, BC: Harbour Publishing, 2009, 43.

22 Schneider, Stephen. *Iced: The Story of Organized Crime in Canada*. Mississauga, ON: Wiley, 1993, 192.

{ The Commodore Ballroom and Granville Street, 1950.
Photo: Art Jones, Vancouver Public Library 83192 }

COME DANCING

Four

Imagine stepping into the Commodore of the 1930s or '40s, walking up the grand staircase into the ballroom, and seeing the band onstage play songs by Count Basie or Tommy Dorsey as the dance floor filled with couples. At tables along the back and sides of the dance floor, groups of friends laughed loudly or held intimate conversations, while uniformed wait staff moved efficiently about the room. Even if you were too old, too young, or too far away to be at the Commodore, you could still revel in the sounds of the evening's entertainment by tuning into a local radio station to hear a "remote," a popular radio trend of the period that broadcasted the house orchestra live, after the evening news.

These were good times to be a musician. Band members could earn ten to twenty dollars a night, which was good money in the 1930s. Work was plentiful, too—in the big band era, orchestras commonly had up to twelve members, before smaller jazz combos later became popular in the 1950s and '60s. But the bands, as good as some of them were, often weren't the main attraction; the rooms themselves were the stars. The house bands and orchestras were a part of the halls

and hotels in which they played, rather than being the primary draw.

Band leader Dal Richards spent twenty-five years at the Hotel Vancouver's Panorama Roof Ballroom (three blocks away from the Commodore). He would come to know many of the other local bandleaders and groups that played around town over the years, including the regular orchestras at the Commodore. Wendell Dorey's orchestra played at the grand re-opening in 1931, and Don Flynn took over as the band leader not long afterward. "Don was a friendly, easy-going guy," Richards recalls. "I sat in with him a few times in gigs in Stanley Park together. Don would stand there on the bandstand conducting while we were playing. He'd be facing us, and he'd say, 'Look at that ugly woman dancing down there,' or 'Look at that big fat fella in the cheap suit in the second row.' He'd point out people in the audience who couldn't hear him and crack us up while we were playing." Bob Lyon took over the stage after Don Flynn and played there regularly through the late '30s before leaving for Australia in 1939.

Nanaimo-born Charlie Pawlett was well-known in town, having played in the pit orchestras at the Orpheum, Pantages, and Capitol Theatres in the 1920s. His band featured at the Commodore until Ole Olsen and His Commodores became the regular house orchestra in the 1940s. "Ole was good, but he lived in Dunbar, so at the end of the night, he was always in a rush to catch a streetcar home," Richards laughs.

After the war, George Calangis and his band played the Commodore through the 1950s. Richards remembers him as a good musician and a member of one of the city's foremost musical families. Calangis and his five sisters had toured the

west coast as the Musical Calangis Family; later, George conducted the Canadian Broadcasting Corporation (CBC) orchestra that appeared on a number of CBC radio programs. When Calangis's vocalist, Lorraine McAllister, left his orchestra in 1950, she joined Richards' band. Richards not only gained a vocalist, but a year later made McAllister his wife.

In the 1950s and '60s, Doug Kirk and his band appeared frequently at the Commodore. Richards recalls that "he wasn't a great musician, but he didn't have to be. Sometimes you could get away with that," and Kirk did so by emceeing many of the functions and parties held at the Commodore during his tenure.

Toward the end of his career in the 1960s, orchestra leader Len Chamberlain, who had played the Crystal Ballroom at the old Hotel Vancouver in the 1930s, performed regularly at the Commodore, as did Dal Richards, but it was Mart Kenney and his Western Gentlemen who played there most often through the decades. "Mart Kenney was the Glenn Miller of Canada," Richards says. "He realized early on the value of radio and got on the radio whenever he could. He started to tour more than any of us." Kenney's band performed on and off at the Commodore from the 1940s until the '70s.

In the early years, bands had an illuminated, hand-cranked rolling sign onstage that listed what dances were next—the Waltz Quadrille, the Fox Trot, the Military Two Step, the Moonlight, or the Home Waltz. Dal Richards recalls that the Lindy Hop, popular in the swing era, never caught on in Vancouver. Hoagy Carmichael's ballad "Stardust" was popular in the 1930s, and by the 1940s, the Glenn Miller instrumental "Tuxedo Junction" was often requested. One popular dance of the day, the Lambeth Walk, was taken from the 1937 musical *Me and My*

Vancouver bandleader Mart Kenney was known as the "Glenn Miller of Canada." He performed at the Commodore for more than three decades. Photo and card: Courtesy of Neptoon Records Archives

The Commodore Cabaret

PRESENT

CANADA'S PREMIER BAND

Mart Kenney

AND HIS ORCHESTRA

ONE NIGHT ONLY

Wednesday, JUNE 12th - Dancing at 9 p.m.

TICKETS NOW ON SALE AT THE COMMODORE

$1.75 EACH, INCLUDING TAX   SUPPER NOT INCLUDED

PAC. 7838

During World War II, the Commodore remained open for various wartime fundraisers. Here, members of the Vancouver Air Raid Precautions committee meet for their annual banquet. Photo: Donn B. A. Williams, December 1944, City of Vancouver Archives CVA 586-3533

Girl, and first performed in Vancouver at the Commodore that same year by Mart Kenney and his Western Gentlemen.[23] With its jaunty strutting style and dancers shouting "Oi!" at the end of each chorus, it became a craze in the 1940s. But when the dance caught on in Germany, one Nazi official called it "Jewish mischief [and] animalistic hopping" and vowed to stamp it out. It would later be a hit for Duke Ellington.[24] Just as rock 'n' roll would later threaten the status quo, in its early days jazz music was believed by some members of society to contribute to "moral leniency."

When World War II began, although Vancouver was not on the front lines, there were fears that it could be a target, especially after the Japanese attack on Pearl Harbor, when Japanese submarines prowled the coast of Vancouver Island. Almost overnight, air raid blackouts and rationing became part of daily life in Vancouver, as did wartime austerity and the notion that recreational pursuits should take a back seat. For most of the war years, the Commodore was open only on Saturday nights, but it found a way to contribute to the war effort as a banquet and meeting hall for wartime fundraisers and social occasions for civil-defense groups such as the annual Air Raid Precaution (ARP) dinners. Although the ARP committee strategically avoided booking their parties on nights scheduled for air raid tests, when sirens signalled emergency blackouts—in which streetlights were turned off and residents were required to put up black-out sheets in their windows and turn off lights in their homes—the Commodore remained open, with its lights out, window blinds drawn, and candles lit at the tables, until the all-clear sign was given. There was no need to completely ruin an evening out just because Vancouver might be attacked.

During the war years, the Commodore also became a popular spot for the University of British Columbia Nurses' Dances, which were held for soldiers preparing to ship out. While these events were full of levity, they were undoubtedly tinged with an unspoken sadness, as some of the soldiers enjoyed their last night in town before shipping overseas, perhaps never to return.

On July 15, 1940, a gala fundraiser was planned at the Commodore with the Air Supremacy Drive in aid of War Savings. This was to be a major social event in the city with all the right people in attendance. RCAF Air Marshal Billy Bishop himself, the Canadian World War I hero and flying ace, was there along with Jackie Souder's Olympic Hotel Orchestra from Seattle.[25] But in the early morning hours of that day, Vancouver police constable Bob Tyldesley, who was patrolling Granville Street, discovered a break-in at the Commodore. The office safe had been blown open by safecrackers who had smashed through a skylight window. In Kogos's office, detectives found two dismantled flashlights and a piece of fuse left behind by the safecrackers. A smaller safe had been carried to the rear steps of the service entrance where it was smashed open. The thieves made off with $650 in cash.[26] The incident made the front page of the *Vancouver Sun*, which blamed "yeggs"—burglars or safecrackers. In the days before debit and credit cards, burglars often targeted theatres and nightclubs because of the large amounts of cash (from tickets and concessions) kept on site. The case went unsolved. Despite the police activity around the Commodore that morning, the Gala was a success. The show must go on.

Despite its size and amenities, the Commodore Cabaret was rarely used as a concert venue in its early days. The Palomar

Top: Constable Bob Tyldesley discovered the break-in at the Commodore. Photo: Courtesy of the Vancouver Police Museum

Bottom: When the Commodore's safe was blown open by "yeggs" (safecrackers) it made front-page headlines in July 1940. Source: *Vancouver Sun*

Special Matinee...THIS SATURDAY

The Commodore Cabaret

Presenting the Greatest
IN PERSON SHOW EVER
FEATURING

RUDY VALLEE

★ The WILL MASTIN TRIO
With
SAMMY DAVIS, JR.
(Capital Recording Star)
THE SENSATIONAL
★ MERCER BROS.
THE FAMOUS FRENCH SCREEN COMEDIENNE
FIFI D'ORSAY
★ GEORGE CALANGIS
And His
16-PIECE ORCHESTRA
With
JULIETTE

2 P.M. $1.00 (Including Tax)

One of the earliest known Commodore posters. Local orchestra leader George Calangis regularly performed there through the 1940s and '50s. Courtesy of Greg MacDonald

Ballroom and the PNE Forum building had the capacity to hold larger concert crowds for high-profile shows, such as Duke Ellington and Louis Armstrong, with some notable exceptions. Rudy Vallée and the Will Mastin Trio, which featured a young Sammy Davis Jr, both played the Commodore in 1948.

Ninety-four-year-old Jean Bain recalls attending some of the Commodore shows of the period. "I remember seeing Vaughn Monroe at the Commodore in the 1940s. He could give me the shivers, even though I was in love with the man who would become my husband," she laughs. "I used to see Mart Kenney there a lot too. He had a wonderful band to dance to. I knew a couple that went every Saturday night to the Commodore. It meant a great deal to a lot of people then." Bain also recalls how different the city was. "On Friday nights, after I finished at Britannia High School, my mother let me and a couple of girlfriends walk all the way downtown to Granville Street from where we lived on East Hastings. We felt perfectly safe. Nobody stopped us! I still get a kick thinking back on those days."

Because the Commodore Cabaret didn't have a liquor license, it was an all-ages venue. Jean Bain's younger sister, Norma Arnett, started to going there when she was about seventeen. "The rest of the crowd was a bit older than I was. I remember seeing the house band Ole Olsen and His Commodores there [in the mid-1940s]. It was a twelve-piece band, and they played jitterbug, some popular music of the day, and also slow songs. Chicken à la King with a buttered bun and some greens seemed like the only thing ever on the menu—but you didn't really come for the dinner," recalls Arnett. It was dancing on the Commodore floor that brought them in when

The Alexandra Ballroom, built in 1922, stood at the southeast corner of Hornby and Robson streets. It was renamed Danceland in 1956 and saw performances by Ike and Tina Turner, the Coasters, and Bobby Darin. Photo: Walter E. Frost, May 1965, City of Vancouver Archives CVA 447-351

Coat-check girls Dorian Christie, Jane Marwick, and
Elise Hartwick, 1949. Photo: Judi Riach, courtesy of
Theota Dancer

the bottle-club days of the Cabaret were in full swing. "You
took your bottle and put it under the table. I never did it, of
course," she says, adopting a particularly prim tone. "But my
date would. The police would come in, but never found anything. As long as people were reasonably behaving themselves
it wasn't a problem."

Vancouverites weren't limited in their choices for an evening out; they could go to the Embassy Ballroom on Davie
Street, the White Lane Ballroom on Broadway, or Danceland
off Robson and Hornby Street. But the Commodore's sprung
floor and its ornate décor set it apart from other places in town.
"We were crazy for dancing," recalls ninety-year-old Mildred
Henderson, who in her late teens used to hop on the Vancouver
streetcars to go to dance spots where she jitterbugged to Glenn
Miller and Tommy Dorsey songs. "The world was different—
and changing. Women didn't wear slacks then, just dresses.
I remember when I got my first pair of slacks—this was in
the '40s—and I walked down Granville Street in them. It sure
turned heads!" Henderson and her husband often met friends
at the Commodore where they could socialize around the large
tables. "It was a classier place with nice people. I remember the
coat-check girls there."

Dorian Christie was just fifteen years old when she started
working at the Commodore as a coat-check clerk in 1946.
"My mother wouldn't let me work there unless somebody
could drive me home at the end of the night," she recalls. Aged
eighty-two and still living in Vancouver, she has vivid memories of her nights at the club in the late '40s. "It was an elegant
place. All these people showed up on Saturday nights—the only
night it was regularly open then—and you could see women

in long dresses and cashmere coats, all the men in tuxes, sometimes even spats. On some busy nights, when we had 1,000 people, the coat check racks nearly overflowed. People waited in long lines to pick up their jackets, umbrellas, or even top hats," she says, describing a scene that Commodore patrons might recognize today.

Christie worked at the coat-check with two other young women, June Marwick and Elsie Hartwig. "June was very good and watched out for me. Her family came from Shaughnessy, and she was married to an engineer. Elsie's family was Italian, and they had a chocolate shop on Commercial Drive." Beyond being instructed to always dress in a black skirt and white blouse, Christie, Marwick, and Hartwig were also given specific rules to follow while working at the Cabaret, which included customer etiquette and not taking tips. "June said we could take some tips, and we'd sometimes hide quarters in our shoes, but if you put too much in there, it hurt your foot. You were supposed to be friendly, but not too friendly. I remember there was one young man, a regular, who often talked to me, and I was polite and friendly—but if I ever gave him my phone number, or went out with him—oh no, I would have been fired," Christie says.

"One time, at a police function at the Commodore, a policeman from Seattle gave me a ten-dollar tip. It was so much, Elsie had to ring it in. I just took a little bit. We'd be too worried about getting fired if we took all the tips we received," she says, still sounding a little worried she might get caught after all these years. It was a good job that she enjoyed, and the staff were paid weekly in cash in little brown envelopes dispensed by Nick Kogos himself. "Mr Kogos was all business," she recalls.

"Usually he wore a tux. At night, he would pinch your arm when you weren't looking, to tease you. I guess that's what men do to girls in Greece. I didn't like that. Mr Kogos's brother, Tony, was the head chef at the Commodore. He treated us well and sometimes had dinner prepared for the staff when we arrived, before starting work. All the Chinese cooks reported to Tony. He always said that his brother better not come into the kitchen and give him any orders, because it was his domain!"

The Cabaret also employed security "Commissionaires" who stood at the top of the stairs "to make sure there weren't any problems." But on one occasion, Christie recalls that security couldn't stop one group of party crashers.

The University of British Columbia Engineers had their faculty dinner event at the Commodore. Some students from the Agricultural faculty crashed the party with live chickens they'd hid in their overcoats. I was working on the front landing at the top of the stairs when these guys ran by me—I couldn't stop them. When they got upstairs, they let loose these chickens onto the dance floor, and it caused a real commotion. I think they thought they'd pull this stunt and leave, taking the chickens back to UBC, but the cooks in the kitchen came running out, chased and caught the chickens, and killed them. They had the chickens practically cooking in the kitchen before these students even knew what had happened.

One might imagine that the Commodore waiters told diners that the Chicken à La King was particularly fresh that night.

Banquets held at the Commodore, c. 1950s.
Photos: Courtesy of Neptoon Records Archives

From the vantage point of the coat check, Christie got to see an impressive roster of people—from Mayors Tom Alsbury and Fred Hume, to local businessmen and popular personalities of the day—walk up those stairs. There were also people she wasn't so sure about.

One night, a bunch of guys came in with their dates. They were dressed up, but sort of overdressed. It was quite the arrival. There was some fuss by Mr Kogos; he wanted to get them the good tables. I asked him if they were the police, and he laughed and said, "No—those aren't the police. Those are the guys that pay the police! Those are the Filippones!" They were the Italian brothers who operated the Penthouse Nightclub. Some of the girls who were their dates were, I think, chorus girls, but we gossiped that they might have even been streetwalkers. I remember [Penthouse Nightclub owner] Joe Philliponi was there with a woman with bright red hair, who was wearing a fox fur with the head still on it. They were pretty flashy. Too much for me.

Although the Saturday night dinner and dancing was popular, private parties continued to form the majority of the Commodore's business. In the mid-1950s, one typical event was the Infants' Ball, the annual fundraiser for the Vancouver General Hospital's children's ward. The list of guests included then-Lieutenant Governor Clarence Wallace, former Lieutenant Governor Eric Hamber, Mayor Fred Hume, and noted local doctor George Frederick Strong, along with a number of hospital directors, university deans, and well-to-do benefactors. There were presentations, dinner, music, and prize giveaways that included gift certificates to local businesses like Eaton's department store and Ingledew's Shoes. The impressive grand prize was a flight for two to Mexico on Canadian Pacific Airlines. In the evening's program, guests could read the description of the exotic and thoroughly modern getaway: "In just ten hours, non-stop by Super DC-6, sunny skies and gay tropic nights welcome you to a vacation. Explore Mexico City, 'Paris of the Americas,' dance in exciting Latin clubs, or thrill to a bullfight, on flights for just $127.50."

To today's readers, the club parties and gatherings at the Commodore may sound like unusually formal and staid functions, but socializing within clubs and fraternal organizations was typically how people gathered in that era. Kogos and Dillias took advantage of the trend, and built a reputation in the city by focusing on functions that kept Rotary Clubs, Toastmasters, Shriners, Masons, Daughters of the Nile, and other fraternal groups and sports associations flocking to the Commodore.

Not everything went as planned. In 1955, Vancouver detective Cecil McCallan, who was attending the annual police sports banquet at the Commodore, died suddenly of a heart attack. He had joined the police department two months before the Commodore opened. Considered a respected member of the department, he'd worked on the dry squad, which had raided the Commodore and other clubs. Some grimly joked that McCallan had done his job so well that the place was finally settling the score. Such was the dark humour that existed in the rivalry between the club owners and the police.

The company banquets provided good, predictable business. By the 1950s, however, a new invention, television, started to keep people at home instead of out on the dance floor on Saturday nights. While other clubs, in response, started to book touring shows from the nightclub circuit, Kogos and Dillias continued to rely on the tried and true.

23 Davis. *The Vancouver Book*, 11.

24 "The Lambeth Walk," *The One Show*, BBC TV, February 7, 2013.

25 "Inspecting New Trainer Plane," *Vancouver Sun*, July 13, 1940, 12.

26 "Yeggs Get into Office by Light Well," *Vancouver Sun*, July 15, 1950, 1.

Souvenir photo card, 1948.
Courtesy of Bill Allman

CKNW'S
"NIGHT OF NIGHTS"
in aid of the
CKNW ORPHANS' FUND
✦
THE "COMMODORE"
✦
April 21st, 1965

{ CKNW Orphans' Fund Evening program, April
21, 1965. Courtesy Neptoon Records Archives }

Five

DEATH AND TAXES AND A LIGHT AT THE END OF THE CAVE

THE DECADE OF the 1950s didn't begin favourably for Nick Kogos. In 1951, he was found guilty of failing to pay the Commodore Cabaret's taxes between 1942 and 1948. He was fined $500 and also had to pay $110,000 in a court settlement. But the 1950s turned out to be good years for the Commodore, and Kogos was able to recover the money he'd lost to the tax man. He was even able to make a substantial contribution to a fundraiser, held at the Commodore, for the victims of the 1953 earthquake in Greece that took the lives of 600 people.

After a lengthy fight with cancer, George Reifel passed away in July 1958. But it was the death of his partner Johnny Dillias in 1959 that really changed things for Kogos. Dillias's wife Marion stayed on to work as the Cabaret's accountant, but Kogos, after thirty years at the Commodore, knew it was time to retire. "Those two were so close," former coat-check clerk Dorian Christie recalls. "They were inseparable. I knew Mr Kogos couldn't go on without Johnny."

The Commodore had made Kogos a wealthy man. After leaving the Commodore, he took a cruise around the

Doug Gourlay at radio KPO–NBC in San Francisco, early 1940s. Photo: Courtesy of Patrick Gourlay

world and retired to his multi-million-dollar home in West Vancouver, where he built his own private Parthenon, complete with large white columns and statues. There, he lived out his days on his little piece of the Athenian Acropolis, right in the middle of the exclusive British Properties neighbourhood.

The man who would take on ownership of the Commodore and lead it through the 1960s came literally from within the Commodore family. Doug Gourlay started his career as a radio announcer at CJOR in Vancouver, becoming the station's chief announcer in 1937. He married Audrey Reifel, the daughter of George C. Reifel, in 1942, before the couple left for the US, where Gourlay took a job at a radio station in Salt Lake City. He also worked in San Francisco and eventually became "chief announcer for NBC in Los Angeles," his son Patrick Gourlay says. "He worked as the announcer on radio shows with Bob Hope, Bing Crosby, Fibber McGee and Molly, and the Bob Burns show. He'd introduce the acts and read the ads."

Doug and Audrey already had a son and daughter when he decided to move to New York at the dawn of the television industry. "But my grandmother Alma [Reifel] begged them to come back to Vancouver," says Patrick Gourlay. Alma Reifel could be persuasive; after all, she'd already convinced her husband to build the Commodore, and she convinced her daughter and son-in-law to return to Vancouver where their youngest son, Patrick, was born in 1953. (Sadly, Audrey died in childbirth; Doug remarried in 1964.) When he returned to Vancouver, Doug began to work at Alberta Distilleries, one of the Reifel's Vancouver-based companies, but after the death of George Reifel and Nick Kogos's retirement, he saw an opportunity to take over the Commodore Cabaret.

Vancouver Sun saloon-beat reporter Jack Wasserman asked readers in an August 17, 1961 column if they were "wondering about the terse note advertising that the Commodore is 'Under New Management,'" and then he revealed that Doug Gourlay was the new owner, who had "put up a guesstimated $75,000 to buy the world's most successful cabaret business."[27]

Patrick Gourlay was given an inauspicious start in show business when he was just eight years old. "My memories of the Commodore are always of Saturday mornings. I would come down with my father, and he'd put me to work wiping down the big brass railings that people had left hand prints all over. Then I'd pick up pop bottles—these were the bottle-club days when they sold just pop and ice to go with the alcohol people brought in and hid away, so there were lots of empties! I suppose I was slave labour for my dad," he laughs, "but I enjoyed it." By the early 1960s, Patrick began to earn some dividends. "We'd spend three or four hours working at the Commodore in the mornings and have lunch there. Bill West was the chef then; he always had a huge tureen of oxtail soup cooking in the Commodore kitchen. Because my grandfather owned some properties on Granville Street, we got free admission at all the theatres there, so once I'd finished work, I'd go watch movies all afternoon," Patrick recalls. "And the Notte family, who ran the Bon Ton Bakery downstairs from the Commodore, used to give us cookies and cakes. We got treated very well!"

Throughout the 1960s, the Commodore remained a popular banquet hall for local clubs and associations, from

Bill West (in chef's hat) was the well-known head chef at the Commodore Ballroom in the 1960s.
Photo: Courtesy of Neptoon Records Archives

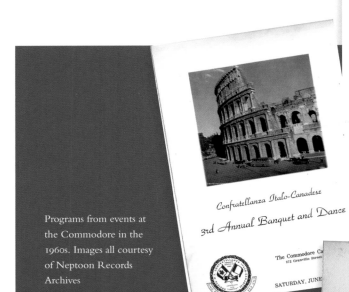

Programs from events at the Commodore in the 1960s. Images all courtesy of Neptoon Records Archives

Confratellanza Italo-Canadese
3rd Annual Banquet and Dance

The Commodore Ca...
872 Granville Street...

SATURDAY, JUNE...

Honoured Guests

Mr. Louis Graziano, Chairman, and Miss Wosko
The Honorable Mr. Justice A. E. Branca, President, and Mrs. Branca
Attilio Gatto, representing the Consul for Italy, and Mrs. Gatto
Alderman R. Atherton, representing His Worship the Mayor, and Mrs. Atherton
Alderman and Mrs. H. Wilson
The Most Reverend Martin M. Johnson, D.D., Archbishop of the Archdiocese of Vancouver
Reverend Father Della Torre
Honourable John Nicholson, O.B.E., M.P.
Honourable Grayce McCarthy, Minister without Portfolio, and Mr. McCarthy
Mr. Herb Capozzi, M.L.A., Vancouver Centre, and Mrs. Capozzi
Mr. Ronald Basford, M.P., and Mrs. Basford
Mr. Lloyd Brown, District Sales Manager C.P.A., and Mrs. Brown
Dr. and Mrs. E. J. Signori
Mr. and Mrs. Marino Culos
Mr. and Mrs. Cadorin
Mr. and Mrs. Primo Tesan
Mr. Rinaldo Torrentino and guest

Honoured Guests to be honoured

Mr. and Mrs. Sam Bass
Mr. and Mrs. Joseph Cohen
Mr. and Mrs. Jack Cohen
Mr. A. G. Duncan Crux
Mr. and Mrs. Robert DeCamillis
Mr. and Mrs. Jack Diamond
Mr. Arthur Fouks, Q.C., and Mrs. Fouks
Mr. and Mrs. Ben Wosk
Mr. and Mrs. Nick Alvaro
Mr. Julius E. Bengert
Mr. Howard S. Marshall
Mr. Joseph J. Custock

COCKTAILS: 6:30 P.M. – 7:00 P.M.

DINNER: 7:00 P.M.

DANCE: 8:00 P.M. TO MIDNIGHT

"A HAPPY TIME TO ALL"

Menu

CHILLED ANTIPASTO

KAMLOOPS ROAST BEEF — NATURAL GRAVY

ROAST POTATOES

BUTTERED GREEN PEAS

HOMEMADE ROLLS   BUTTER

INDIVIDUAL MOCHA CAKES

COFFEE OR TEA

Luncheon

Tendered by the Government and the People of the Province of British Columbia to the

Canadian Dental Association
61st ANNUAL MEETING

COMMODORE CABARET
Vancouver, B.C.

MONDAY, JUNE 4, 1962

E. SARTAIN

Menu

HEARTS OF CELERY AND ASSORTED OLIVES

CRABMEAT COCKTAIL

PACIFIC SPRING SALMON SALAD

ROLLS AND BUTTER

PIE

COFFEE

C.A.P.A. —

British Columbia District

Wish All Their Friends

A Very Merry Christmas

And A

Happy New Year

Christmas Party

Commodore Cabaret • Friday, Dec. 15th

C.A.P.A. – British Columbia District

MENU

Chilled Antipasto

Kamloops Roast Beef — natural gravy

Roast Potatoes

Cut Green Beans

Homemade Rolls and Butter

Individual Mocha Cakes

Coffee or Tea

PROGRAMME

Introduction and Welcome
Roy E. Davidson
President,
C.A.P.A. — British Columbia District

Floor Show — Kristmas Kapers

DAL RICHARDS
Master of Ceremonies

DELOVLIES — Chorus Line

JUDY GINN — Beauty in Song

CAROL KEATH — Acrobatics

LEON WARRICK — Great Entertainer

Dancing to the music of
Dal Richards and His Orchestra

CHAIRMAN
DR. WILLIAM MILLER, PRESIDENT

TOAST TO THE QUEEN

GREETINGS FROM OFFICIAL REPRESENTATIVES

GREETINGS AND ADDRESS
THE HONORABLE R. W. BONNER, Q.C.,
Attorney-General and
Minister of Industrial Development, Trade, and Commerce

ADDRESS BY PRESIDENT MILLER

PRESENTATION OF HONORARY MEMBERSHIP
REPLY BY HONORARY MEMBER

INSTALLATION OF NEW PRESIDENT
REMARKS BY NEW PRESIDENT

PRESENTATION OF PAST PRESIDENT'S JEWEL

ADJOURNMENT

Programme

the Confratellanza dinners (gatherings of businessmen from the local Italian-Canadian community), to benefits for the CKNW Orphans' Fund, and the Sport of Kings soirées for thoroughbred racehorse owners from Vancouver's Exhibition Park racecourse. Gourlay also started a once-a-month luncheon at the Commodore called the Touchdown Club. "All the BC Lions would show up," Patrick says. "These were the days of Willie Fleming and Joe Kapp. You could meet the team, get autographs, have a few drinks, and go back to work."

He also remembers stories of some wild nights. "Mardi Gras parties at the Commodore—these were big nights. At one of them, a guy who came dressed as a Viking later passed out drunk somewhere in the ballroom, where nobody noticed him. Sometime after they'd turned off the lights and closed up for the night, he woke up. After stumbling around in the dark, still drunk, he finally kicked open a door. He'd already triggered the alarm, and the police showed up to find this drunk Viking trying to break *out* of the Commodore."

During Doug Gourlay's ownership, he renovated the Commodore's interior, putting in new carpets and drapes and updating the decor of the room. Saturday night dinner and dancing continued with Mart Kenney and His Western Gentlemen and Dal Richards' Orchestra, but the city's night-life was changing, and there was more competition for audiences. The focus of Vancouver's entertainment scene had shifted two blocks west of the Commodore to Hornby Street and to the unlikely interior of a Cave.

In the 1960s, while the Commodore's ballroom floor was still the best place in town for dancing, the Cave Supper Club at 626 Hornby was the spot to see a show. The club, which opened in 1937, was decorated with imitation stone walls and large stalactites made from painted burlap and papier-mâché. The cavernous space had an exotic appeal, and the club grew in popularity when it began to book some of the more sophisticated acts of the post-war years, such as Lena Horne. For her 1946 appearance at the Cave, she was paid $7,500 for the week—the highest fee for a club show in Vancouver to date. Dal Richards recalled being in attendance for one of her performances; that event, he later realized, signalled a change for Vancouver nightclubs. "By show time, the crowd stretched from the Hornby Street entrance up the block to the Hotel Georgia. Someone was sent out to nab the club's regulars and sneak them down the lane and in through the back door. I knew the headwaiter, and got a ringside seat. I was twenty-eight years old. Lena was show-stopping gorgeous. I have never had a bigger thrill than watching that show. It was a triumph, and it opened the door for a stream of big acts that made Vancouver a stop for the next two decades."[28]

When the Cave received one of British Columbia's first club liquor licenses in 1954, it became *the* place to go. The two-level nightclub could seat 850 people, but on busy nights, easily pushed a standing-room-only capacity to 1,000. Between the hundreds of dinners served each night and the legions of Mad Men buying drinks for themselves and their dates, the Cave could well afford to bring in some of the biggest names on the circuit. Audiences in the smoky confines of the Hornby Street club saw acts such as Ray Charles, Diana Ross and the Supremes, Louis Prima and Sam Butera, Stan Getz, Tony Bennett, Frankie Laine, Buddy

Diners at the Commodore, c. 1950s. Photo: W.G. McLuckie, courtesy of Neptoon Records Archive

Rich, Oscar Peterson, Anthony Newley, Johnny Cash, and Sonny and Cher—all frequently backed by Cave bandleader Fraser MacPherson and his orchestra—or comedians such as Don Rickles and Jack Carter. Entertainers Mitzi Gaynor and Rolf Harris were mainstays. And if that night's Cave show didn't interest Vancouverites, Isy's Supper Club and Oil Can Harry's were within walking distance, where touring jazz and soul artists often performed.

Throughout the 1960s, the Commodore continued to host staff banquets, company parties, and social club dinners. Look at photographs of typical Commodore patrons of this era and you'll see the older, more serious faces of those who'd been through the Depression and World War II dancing to the old chestnuts, while younger, less formal, and more hip crowds were having all the real fun over at the Cave and other clubs. Despite the renovations that Gourlay had made to the room, the Commodore was beginning to feel out of step with the times, as if it was for the Eisenhower generation, while the Kennedys were living it up at the Cave.

Gourlay's own musical tastes were shaped by the big band years—he'd met many of the era's biggest performers during his radio days. But with kids of his own playing the Rolling Stones and Beatles, Gourlay was prescient enough to know that the music and culture were changing, and it was time to open up the room to a new generation of promoters and party organizers.

Perhaps Drew Burns seemed to be just another new face looking to book the Commodore from Gourlay in the mid-1960s. But Burns wasn't representing a Women's Auxiliary wanting to hold a fundraiser or a local chapter of the Knights of Columbus planning to organize a banquet. He represented a new way that men and women in Vancouver were meeting each other, and it would quickly become his full-time job and allow him to make an indelible and invaluable contribution to the city's cultural and artistic growth.

....

27 Wasserman, Jack. "The Town Around Us," *Vancouver Sun,* August 17, 1961.

28 Richards and Taylor, *One More Time,* 100.

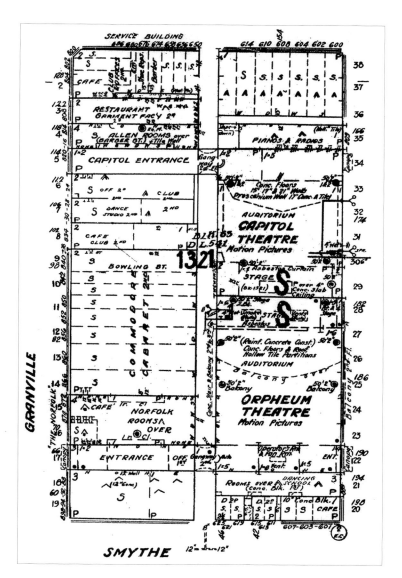

The January 1955 fire insurance map details the 800 block of Granville Street. City of Vancouver Archives, CVA Map 610

Six

THANK DREW IT'S FRIDAY

Born in Winnipeg in 1933 and raised in a very religious Pentecostal family, Drew Burns came to Vancouver in the 1950s and first went to the Commodore as an eighteen-year-old for a family banquet. For a time, he worked as a textiles salesman, but aside from a stint in the choir for Theatre under the Stars, he had no experience in show business or nightclub management. Burns was a man with strong instincts and an often ribald sense of humour, though perhaps his best skill was knowing how to make sure people had a good time. It was inevitable, therefore, that before long, he would find the kind of job in which he could exploit that talent. He certainly knew how to have a good time himself.

In the 1950s and early '60s, Burns didn't have the money to catch all of his favourite jazz musicians, such as Woody Herman or Stan Kenton, who regularly played at the Cave and other nightclubs, so he devised his own methods for getting through the front door. "I'd put on a suit and borrow my older brother's trumpet case," he recalls. "There was never anything inside the case, but nine times out of ten they'd let me through."

Vancouver, like other cities throughout North America in the 1960s, saw increasingly open-minded attitudes about relationships between the sexes. The way men and women met and mingled was changing; young people had more options and were no longer limited to socializing solely with those in their high school or college circles. By the late '60s, as the hippies started to enjoy the fruits of the free-love movement, the "average" guy or girl, who didn't necessarily fit in with the Kitsilano Beach Be-In crowd, were looking for ways to get together as well.

Capitalizing on changing times, in 1966 Burns teamed up with businessman Grayson Hand to form a new venture. Hand had money to invest thanks to the success of his company Tasco, Vancouver's first phone-answering service. It employed banks of receptionists to field telephone calls long before the days of mobile phones or even cassette answering machines for people—particularly business executives—who paid to have a round-the-clock contact number where messages could be left and retrieved. Social networking and Internet dating were inconceivable, so bringing people together required a different set of strategies. Burns started a singles club in Vancouver called the Fifth Day Club, open only to single men and women (although there were no background checks). For five dollars, participants got a gold membership card that gave them access to various social events, including Friday night parties, weekend ski trips, and Grey Cup football games. "We didn't have our own venue," said Burns, "but we started holding parties at the Bayshore Hotel and Hotel Vancouver and bringing in big crowds. Our staff wore navy blue pants and a good jacket with a crest that read 'Mr. Goodlife.' It was unique at the time

because only the dreary hotel beer parlours were around," said Burns. They received plenty of promotion for the Fifth Day Club right away, "because we made all the local radio DJs honorary members, and that got them talking about it on-air."

One of the first Fifth Club Day events "was held at the Commodore in 1966," recalled Burns. "It didn't have a liquor license yet, but I got a one-night permit. That night, when the doors opened at 8:00 p.m., there was nobody there. At 9:00 p.m., it was still dead, and I started to worry. I mean, there was nobody. All of a sudden, at 10:00, they all flooded in." Burns had packed the Commodore on his first try.

While young Vancouver men and women had found new ways to relax and meet one other, the province's liquor laws were also slowly relaxed, and the first liquor licenses were issued for cocktail lounges and restaurants. Some cabarets that had operated for more than twenty years were finally being granted licenses to legally sell alcohol. The downtown nightclubs began to enjoy new crowds of young singles seeking places to socialize over drinks and dancing. "All of a sudden, nightclub owners realized that single people had the money," Burns says.

Danny Baceda, owner of the popular Vancouver nightclub Oil Can Harry's, was interviewed in the University of British Columbia's campus newspaper, *The Ubyssey*, in October 1968. "In Vancouver, the West End has done tremendous things to a man's sex life," he told the paper. "These high rises, with literally hundreds of unattached young people and no parents standing around pointing their fingers at you, has done wonders. You have two guys living in an apartment, and two girls in another. You have one guy going into the girls' and one

COMMODORE CABARET   SEPT. 67

Vancouver had never seen anything quite like the Fifth Day Club. Photos: Courtesy of Neptoon Records Archives

COMMODORE CABARET

THE FIFTH DAY →

Fifth Day Club. Photo: Courtesy
of Neptoon Records Archives

girl going into the guys'—just to watch television together. But all sorts of things can happen and they do." The article had the eyebrow-raising headline "Virgin Hunting in the Concrete Jungle" and featured candid interviews with young, single women who worked in Vancouver. It offered a revealing look at how times were changing for the very audience that Burns' Fifth Day Club had capitalized upon. "The working girl today appears to be more sophisticated and more sexually knowledgeable than the working girl of your mother's generation," the article stated. "And it isn't easy to find a twenty-one-year-old virgin. The Pill has come to replace the daily vitamin. Shocking? Maybe. But a more accurate word would be realistic. Downtown, a twenty-one-year-old girl who is a virgin is a surprise. People no longer question whether the boy and girl seeing one another for longer than four months are sleeping together, but merely assume they do."[29]

Amidst the young office secretaries and assistants, Drew Burns, then in his early thirties, was also interviewed for the article. He discussed the "phenomenal success" of the Fifth Day Club and noted that, within two years, the club's membership had grown to 4,000 members. "This isn't a lonely hearts club," Burns stressed, noting that couples were not admitted and club membership directories did not print addresses. "There are lots of swingers here. We have doctors, nurses, school teachers, [and] television announcers." And with a description of the Fifth Day Club parties that foreshadowed Burns' future, he said: "There are drinks, tables spread around a dance floor, a live band, and a surprising number of attractive men and women." Photographs of the Fifth Day Club parties capture what this late-1960s downtown Vancouver party scene was like for the young men and women who were not a part of the city's burgeoning hippie happenings in Kitsilano.

Burns began to fill the local venues with parties unlike any the city had seen before. Young men in skinny neckties and blazers danced with young women in bouffant hairstyles. Even the wallflowers were three martinis in, and nearly everyone had a cigarette in hand. If, just a couple of years before, Friday nights for Vancouver's young professionals had meant coming home after work, putting up their feet, and watching the boring glow of the television, now, thanks to Drew Burns, Fridays were something to look forward to. The Fifth Day Club would, according to Burns, become the most popular singles club in North America, growing to 15,000 members.

Burns garnered more local media attention. A *Vancouver Sun* feature noted that the Fifth Day Club "taps the huge well of loneliness and boredom among young business and professional people who live in concrete canyons of the West End and work all week among the settled and married of Coquitlam and Kerrisdale." The *Sun* quoted a female Fifth Day member who said: "If you think you're going to meet your knight in shining armour, forget it. But you get to meet people. Interesting people. It's the greatest thing that's happened to me since I came to Vancouver."

"People are mentally lazy," Burns told the *Sun*. "We have young professional people here who are active—[they] race cars, ski, sail. But on their own, they won't get to work and meet people. If you organize the party, they'll come to it."[30] And organizing the parties is what Burns did.

Even more difficult than organizing the excursions was making sure that everyone made it back to Vancouver. Photo: Courtesy of Neptoon Records Archives

Drew Burns organized seven chartered flights of Fifth Day Club singles on weekend trips to Las Vegas. Photo: Courtesy of Neptoon Records Archives

I took seven chartered aircraft to Las Vegas full of singles. Nobody had ever taken four, never mind seven, before. I had buses to take the club members out to the airport, and I had to be on the first plane to be there when everybody arrived in Vegas. It was chaos because, the couple of days we were there, so many [men and women] went missing, ending up in each other's rooms [where] they weren't initially assigned, [and] we didn't know where any given person was. Then, I had to be on the last plane back with the passenger list to make sure we didn't leave anybody behind because there were so many hung-over stragglers. Everybody had a great time, but I had to stay pretty sober for the whole damn thing just to try to keep an eye on everybody.

Meanwhile, having been at the Commodore for nearly nine years, Doug Gourlay, then in his late fifties, was beginning to feel that it was time to move on. Marion Dillias, still working as the Commodore's office manager, later recalled that, in the late 1960s, Gourlay would leave town for the entire summer and get Dillias to manage things. "He had a great time with [the Commodore]," says Patrick Gourlay of his father. "But I think he had had too many late nights, and it was time to sell."

Doug Gourlay also knew that times were changing. "Doug had been watching what I was doing. He decided that I should have the Commodore," Burns said. "He told me what he wanted for it. I said, 'It was nice talking to you,' and walked away, but he came back with another offer... 'Look at the space. Where are you gonna find space like this in downtown Vancouver?' That was his argument." So with investor assistance from Rob Tyrell, who would become the Commodore's bar manager, and Grayson Hand, who had been involved with the Fifth Day Club, a deal was put together. In November 1969, they purchased the lease from Gourlay.

The night that Burns picked up the keys, he got to do something that few people have been able to do—stand alone in the Commodore, in silence. "You'll find lots of people who've been in the Commodore with a full house, but there are very few people who have been in the room all by themselves. I stood there thinking, *What am I going to do with this place?* I did that a lot in the beginning."

Drew Burns at the Commodore's 50th anniversary party, December 1979.
Photo: Glenn Baglo, *Vancouver Sun*

29 Lee, Bonita. "Virgin Hunting in the Concrete Jungle," *The Ubyssey*, October 18, 10.

30 Down, Audrey. "Leisure Goes to a Party," *Vancouver Sun*, June 13, 1969.

{ Drew Burns in his office at the Commodore,
August 1975. Photo: Glenn Baglo, *Vancouver Sun* }

IT'S SAFE TO say that if someone like Drew Burns, with the energy and vision to navigate the Commodore into a new era, hadn't come along, the club might have closed, been converted to a different business, or suffered demolition, as was the fate of many of the city's now lost or forgotten ballrooms such as the Trianon, the White Rose, and the Pender. During the 1970s and '80s, Vancouver would undergo substantial growth and renewal and often seemed hasty to replace the old with the new, especially when it came to historic buildings. By the early 1970s, the Commodore was considered a nostalgic place, a remnant of a bygone era that hadn't changed in decades. In a *Vancouver Sun* feature that appeared in 1973, reporter Kay Kendall noted that it was the kind of place where you might "run into someone you know. Or someone you used to know, or someone you used to be."[31]

A number of the staff had been there for decades. No one was employed at the Commodore longer than Marion Dillias, who'd been there since the 1930s, diligently working in the office, and maintaining the ballroom books and accounts. And waitresses Jo-Ann Mikeli, Sheila Schellenberg, and Ruby

Anderson, as well as second chef Huey Chai, spent the better part of their working lives there. Olive Mills had worked at the Commodore as a waitress since 1949. "The Commodore had class—you know, prestige," Mills told the *Sun* reporter. "You didn't get rough in the Commodore, and we didn't see much of the permissive [side of] society there."

J.A. "Pops" Wilson, the Commodore's head *maître d'*, was ninety years old in 1973. He'd left the Royal Alexander Hotel in Winnipeg in 1933 (two years after Drew Burns was born) to work at the Commodore, and he'd been there ever since, except for a tour of duty in the merchant navy during World War II. "Pops Wilson was of the old school," recalled Burns. "Putting the wine glasses in exactly the right spot on the table, knowing when things should and shouldn't be served, handling customers—you don't see that these days, even in the high-end places. He was an old-school professional waiter." A balding, bespectacled, urbane man who always wore a jacket, vest, and large bow-tie while at work, Wilson spoke nine languages, knew every rule of etiquette, and treated each of his customers—from the aristocrat to labourers with dirt under their fingernails—with equal respect. He also knew how to deal with difficult situations; once, the story goes, he put an obnoxious youth at an after-grad party in his place by pouring a jug of ice water over his head.

When Burns took over the Commodore in 1969, the venue still did not have a liquor license, so he operated for a time under the old bottle-club rules and sold pop and ice to patrons. "The ice buckets were ceramic bowls," Burns recalled. "We'd charge a buck and half for a bucket of ice. But we'd keep the bowls warm by putting them on top of the oven—they

wouldn't feel hot to the touch, but people would order ice, go out onto the dance floor for two or three songs, and by the time they got back to their table, the ice had half melted. That's how we had to make money back then."

Upon taking ownership, Burns did renovations, removing some of the more garish decorations as well as the plush, curtained booths that lined the walls. But one of his first orders of business was to change the establishment's name from the Commodore Cabaret to the Commodore Ballroom to disassociate the venue from the term "cabaret," which to some now connoted "strip bar," as many "exotic dancing" cabarets were beginning to open all over town.

During Burns' first years, company parties and banquet functions still formed the backbone of the business, although he also brought his Fifth Day Club events into the Commodore regularly. Burns began to keep an eye on local clubs like the Cave, Oil Can Harry's, and the Marco Polo to discern which popular music acts brought in audiences. At first, he hired local groups that he'd booked for Fifth Day Club parties, cover and dance bands like the Night Train Revue, the Wicked Orange, or the Silver Chalice Revue, that played rock and soul music. Burns' ears were open to new sounds, too; he hired the Trinidad Moonlighters Steel Band, fronted by Wilson Wong Moon, who'd immigrated from Trinidad in the 1950s and brought the first authentic sounds of the Caribbean to Vancouver.

The first rock 'n' roll show at the Commodore was in July 1971. Billed as "Mitch Ryder and Detroit," it had a stripped-down version of Ryder's blue-eyed-soul show band, the Detroit Wheels, who had backed his early hits "Devil in a Blue Dress" and "Sock It to Me" and featured a horn section and young

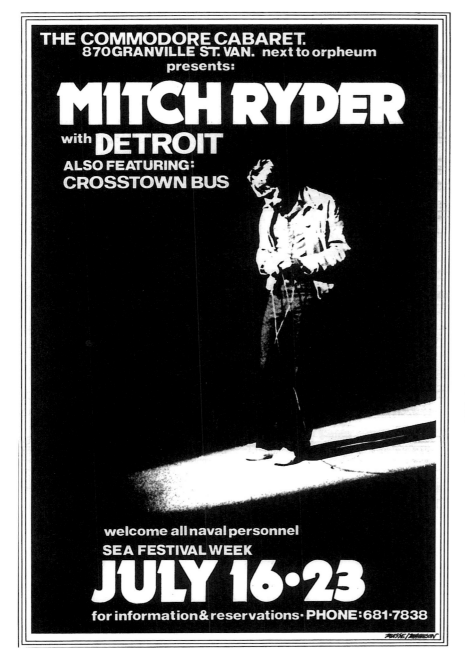

Mitch Ryder's July 1971 show was the first "rock concert" at the Commodore Ballroom. Poster: Courtesy of Neptoon Records Archives

Local band Crosstown Bus opened for Mitch Ryder in July 1971. The band still performs today. Photo: Courtesy of Brian Anderson

female back-up singers. For the opening act, Burns booked Crosstown Bus, a local band he knew from the Fifth Day Club. The crowd in attendance that night was a far cry from the ladies in long satin dresses and mink stoles and the Brylcreemed men in tuxedos who had patronized the Commodore for the previous forty years.

"The place was absolutely packed, and there were all these hippies sitting on the floor," recalls Crosstown Bus lead singer and guitarist Jeff Boyne. "We came out and started to play. People were hooting and really got into it. The dressing rooms backstage were so small that we got to meet the other band and socialize … I think some of Mitch's people were worried that he was too loaded to play the show, but—I'll never forget it—when he got out there, and they started to play, man, oh man, he suddenly kicked in and caught on fire and boy, did he have chops."

Crosstown Bus bassist Brian Anderson recalls that not everyone in the audience, however, enjoyed their music. "My girlfriend at the time—my wife now—had a bunch of relatives visiting from the Prairies, and they came down to the show. They had no idea who we or Mitch Ryder were. So mixed in with all the hippies there was a little crowd of fifty-some-thing aunts and uncles. My wife's aunt said afterward that she thought the music was too loud and she couldn't understand the lyrics, but she was fascinated that when the hippies got up to dance, they didn't need partners to dance with and just sort of moved around on their own. She'd never seen that before."

Anderson later recognized that the Mitch Ryder gig "was a turning point for the Commodore. I didn't realize the significance of the gig at the time and how important it would be

to the rock music scene, but I do remember people saying that Drew was taking 'a hell of a risk' turning it into a rock venue. Thankfully, he saw the opportunity." Despite the big crowd, Burns lost money on the show because he had to pay a high guarantee as Ryder's contracted fee to the band. Still, Burns began to see the future of the Commodore. "I planned it out in my mind, dreaming about all the acts I would like to see in this room that could hold 1,000 people."[32]

At the same Mitch Ryder show, twenty-one-year-old Paul Mercs was one of the people in the crowd who enjoyed the night. Not long afterward, he left Vancouver to "bum around" Europe before finding work as a stagehand for legendary British concert promoter Freddy Bannister's Bath Festival of Blues and Progressive Music that featured Pink Floyd, Santana, and Led Zeppelin. Returning to Vancouver in 1973, Mercs considered becoming a concert promoter after being urged by a friend to put on some events. There were few promoters in Vancouver; large concerts at the Pacific National Exhibition Agrodome and Garden Auditorium were frequently staged by companies in Seattle. Mercs knew about an American band that was touring through the Pacific Northwest and, reminded of the Mitch Ryder show two years earlier, thought he'd try to book them at the Commodore, which, he says, "reminded me of the Lyceum Ballroom in London. So I went to talk to Drew about putting on a show there. [Burns' business partners] Grayson Hand and Rob Tyrell were there too. I had never met any of them before, and they looked at me like I was from Mars. I mean, I was a hippie, and those guys were definitely not from the same generation! I was surprised they didn't say no, but they gave me an 'If you think you can do it…' kind of

Captain Beefheart poster; Ad in the
Georgia Straight, March 1973. Courtesy
of Neptoon Records Archives

response." So, with eleven days to the show date, Mercs booked Captain Beefheart and His Magic Band at the Commodore.

Tickets went on sale, and Mercs placed an advertisement in that week's *Georgia Straight*, the city's counterculture weekly. At local CKLG radio, he cut a promotional spot with legendary station DJ J.B. Shayne. Within days, he'd sold out not one but two nights at the Commodore (Friday, March 2 and Saturday, March 3, 1973). "I put [the band] up at the Holiday Inn on Howe Street," Mercs recalled, "and I went to the hotel the night before the show to see them. The Captain, Don Van Vliet, was great—he had a real intensity. I had a nice chat with him, but I don't know if I understood that much!"

The *Georgia Straight* looks very different today than it did in 1973 when its pages teemed with counterculture reports on marijuana crackdowns, stories of censorship by "the establishment" and controversial police actions, articles about how to make free payphone calls, and ads for hippie clothing stores and mail-order companies that sold stainless steel cocaine straws. The paper also reviewed local concerts and sent a reviewer to the Beefheart show at the Commodore. While the first night was considered "a little ragged," on Saturday night, they brought the house down. "The Captain radiated all manner of evilness," said the unnamed reviewer, and the band "laid down a couple of the most energetic high caliber sets heard in these parts for some time." Starting the set with the song "Pompadour Swamp" that segued into "Low Yo Yo Stuff," guitarist "Zoot Horn Rollo cut loose a few slashing bottleneck chords, and the audience began to shake," noted the *Straight's* reviewer.

This was full throttle rock and roll with plenty of funk and boogie. Saturday night's set had people standing on tables and chairs in order to see anything above the shaking tumult on the dance floor. In fact, the only complaints about the whole affair were from the people who couldn't see—take note, those who were standing on tables because there were those wishing terminal 'things' upon you ... they paid their four bucks too.

At the end of each number there was plenty of applause—mixed with shouts of "Sit down, Assholes!" directed at those standing on tables—and increasing numbers of blitzed looking faces with jaws gone slack. A quick sortie around the premises revealed people collapsed on chairs, tables, and floor, heads still nodding and mouths wide open. Those not bordering on catatonic states indicated the music was "amazing" while others just smiled and went back to the music. Some kind of experience was happening and that's something too many rock concerts seem to lack.[33]

Beefheart closed out the night with two encores. It's difficult to imagine what the Commodore staff—most of whom were used to dealing primarily with bar mitzvahs and banquets—might have thought of the thousand longhaired, oddball Captain Beefheart fans that descended on the Ballroom that weekend. The new "permissive society" that veteran ballroom staff like Olive Mills had happily managed to avoid was now within Commodore's hallowed halls. But the *Georgia Straight* reviewer prophesized: "There will be more shows [like this] coming to the Commodore Ballroom ... and if the Beefheart concert was any indication they should be well worth attending… Hopefully, last weekend's concert will give [the Commodore's management] incentive to keep the shows coming because it's not too often that people in Vancouver manage to combine the elements of good music, good surroundings, and good facilities."

With the Captain Beefheart concert, Paul Mercs' career in the concert business was off and running, and over the next forty years, Mercs continued to bring many more shows to the Commodore and other Vancouver venues, working with acts from Heart to Pearl Jam. He now looks back fondly on his first show there, and is grateful that Drew Burns gave him a chance. "I was just innocent and naïve enough to think I could make it all work. I really didn't know what I was doing, and maybe I still don't," he laughs, "but Drew was great, and it was a great show."

Today, the backstage riders of most rock 'n' roll bands more often contain requests for organic coconut water than Jack Daniel's, and tour managers more frequently inquire where the nearest vegan restaurant is than if the "snowman" is in town; the image of the rock star as a drugged-up, vodka-swilling longhair in leather pants has been a cartoon and caricature for longer than it might ever have been a reality, and to today's youth, the concept of rebellion may be better personified by CIA whistleblower Edward Snowden's thumb drive than by the power and intent of a guitar. Rock music means something different than it did in the 1970s, when it was still a menace to polite society—especially when it was often androgynous, transgressive, and liberating, and definitely not your parents' music.

In 1974, Daniel McNeil was twenty years old and living in the Vancouver suburb of Burnaby when he heard that the New York Dolls were coming to the Commodore. "I read about them in *Rolling Stone*," he recalls. "It was an interesting time, right between glam rock and punk rock, and [the Dolls] filled that void. It was very new and different." McNeil made the New York Dolls' sold-out show along with an audience who'd got into the spirit of the evening by adorning themselves in glitter and feather boas, along with a solid turnout of Vancouver's own drag queen community, including two who came carrying their dates—mannequins dressed in tuxedos. "Drag shows were starting to be pretty common," recalls McNeil. "We were pretty open then; that was the way it was. We used to go to the gay clubs, like Faces at Seymour and Robson, back then, even though we weren't gay, because they had the best dance music and sound systems… I would wear makeup and platform shoes. You have to remember this wasn't long after Davie Bowie's Ziggy Stardust period."

Not everyone at the Dolls' show was a fan. *Vancouver Province* rock critic Jeani Read wrote in her review:

The New York Dolls are two million dollars' worth of hype, and two cents' worth of talent. They have a song called Trash, and that describes them perfectly.

I didn't have the faintest idea what I was doing there. It was all just incomprehensible to me, this weird group of musicians dressed in every grungy imitation of every glitter-theatre-gay shtick imaginable, feather and paint and guns and bracelets and high heels and satin and shimmer stockings, this group of unspeakably crummy aspiring punk-rockers, with a lead singer pretending to be Mick Jagger pretending to be Lou Reed, delivering a performance

The New York Dolls
at the Commodore,
March 13, 1974.
Photos: Courtesy of
Dan McNeil

that didn't even have a vestige of the saving grace of humor,
of the ironic absurdity of their totally ridiculous musical and
or theatrical stance ... If glitter rock isn't dead yet, groups
like The Dolls are definitely going to kill it.[34]

But reviewer Don Stanley from the *Vancouver Sun* had an altogether different take on the show, and on Vancouver audiences:
"I thought I'd die when the Dolls cancelled out last December,"
he wrote. "My only chance gone to see Vancouver's parochial,
super-straight, bourgeois world touched by the magic trash of
New York. I'm so sick of these local, ersatz, country-crooners
and white kiddies blues bands. And when you see touring bub-
blegummers like ELP, Loggins and Messina, and Elton John
(!) getting rave reviews from the local hacks, you know that
nobody in this benighted city knows that New York is where
it's all happening, where it's always happened."[35]

John Mackie, another *Vancouver Sun* reviewer, later recalled
of the Dolls' show that "in those days there was no Internet
and rock bands weren't on television. Because you never got to
see them, to actually be like ten feet away and go 'oh my God
these people really exist'... It was a real event."[36]

Eighteen-year-old John Armstrong had yet to become
known as Buck Cherry, lead singer and guitarist for the
Vancouver's legendary punk-pop combo the Modernettes,
when he went to see the Dolls at the Commodore. (Armstrong
had previously tried to see a Willie Dixon show there, but
without ID was denied entry, and listened to the show from
the sidewalk, thanks to the building's open windows.) "That
show was a huge thing. And it was such a cool place—I'd
never seen a place like that. I remember that my mother was

okay with me going [to the Commodore] because she'd been there with my dad; to her, it was a nice establishment. What could happen in a nice place like that?" Mrs Armstrong likely couldn't even picture what her son was witnessing that night.

> I remember [Dolls' guitarist] Sylvain throwing his feather boa out into the crowd, and a friend of mine caught it. Johnny Thunders teetered about in platform shoes, really fucked-up. I remember thinking that pills, alcohol, and really tall platform shoes are a bad combination. I'd also never seen a band that was legitimately fucked-up onstage before, and it was great. They were indescribably cool, and David Johansen was uproariously funny as a front man—but they were clearly from a different universe.
>
> My [high school] graduation was at the Commodore. Heart was playing. It must have been one of the last gigs they did playing high school graduations before they took off. But I didn't go; seeing the New York Dolls kind of ensured I'd skip my graduation.

Within a few years, Armstrong would be playing onstage at the Commodore himself.

Mart Kenney's big band rang in the New Year on December 31, 1974. It was one of his final Commodore appearances in a career spanning more than thirty-five years on its stage. Just days after the streamers and popped balloons had been swept away, the audience at the Commodore witnessed a show that Kenney and his audience could hardly have imagined.

New York City's KISS, already known for its "blood spitting theatrics," had been touring for just a year when the group

Under-aged John Armstrong was denied entry to a 1975 appearance of Willie Dixon (above) at the Commodore. Photo: Courtesy of Charles Campbell

Mart Kenney, December 31, 1974.
Photos: Courtesy of Neptoon
Records Archives

arrived at the Commodore on January 9, 1975. The band's second album, *Hotter than Hell*, was released three months earlier, but the group had yet to receive the international notoriety it would start to enjoy by the end of that same year, after the release of their live album *Alive!*

Kim Barnatt, then seventeen years old, vividly remembers the evening KISS played the Commodore. "The band had a roadie who must have been about six-foot-five and 270 pounds," Barnatt says. "He walked over to one of the Marshall stack guitar amps and didn't even grab the handles, just slapped his hands on the sides, picked it up, walked it over to the other side of the stage, and plunked it down. I know how heavy those guitar amp stacks are—I couldn't believe it! A few years later, I found out that this was one of KISS's things—they had some empty speaker stacks without wires or speakers; they were just for show to make the band look bigger." Barnatt continues:

When the band came on, they put on a good show, but there were only a few hundred people there—it wasn't sold out…A lot of the bigger shows we went to—Pink Floyd, Yes, and others—were held in the Pacific Coliseum in Vancouver or the Kingdome in Seattle, and you'd be so far away [from the band], it wouldn't really matter where you were. But at the Commodore, you saw bands up close. I distinctly remember Gene Simmons breathing fire. And later on during the show, when Simmons spit blood, a young kid took off his jean jacket and held it out, and Gene just sprayed it, covered it in fake blood. The kid went crazy.

KISS at the Commodore, January 9, 1975.
Photos: Courtesy of Kim Barnatt

What Barnatt captured in his photographs that night are rare glimpses of the early, rudimentary elements of the band live; they look more like a KISS tribute band playing a high school auditorium than the stadium act that the band would soon become.

Touring rock bands were a new trend at the Commodore, but Vancouver groups also got a turn onstage. Popular local bands, entrenched in West Coast blues and folk music, made up the predominant music scene in the early and mid-1970s. "There was a fairly vibrant local band scene then," says Luther Fairbairn of Vancouver's Ambleside Blues Band. "There was Little Daddy and the Bachelors, Jason Hoover and the Epics, the Shantelles, the Shockers, and the Nocturnals, as well as bigger groups like Painted Ship. On the North Shore there were the Burner Boys and a band from the reserve called Whitefeather. But there wasn't yet a lot of live entertainment at the bars in the city. We used to play a place called Club 140 on the North Shore, and there were a few clubs downtown like the Living Room or the Egress on Beatty Street." The Ambleside Blues Band found a regular home on the Commodore stage starting in 1973. "We played the Commodore on bills with the Danny Tripper Band and the Cement City Cowboys a fair bit," recalls Fairbairn.

While Fairbairn fondly recalls playing at the Commodore, he has vivid and less happy memories of what it was like to tour in the rest of the province in the early 1970s. "In Prince George, we looked totally out of place," he says. "I stopped to ask for directions at a Legion. It was the middle of the afternoon, and I walked up to the bar. There were about six guys in there, and the bartender said to me, 'Get the fuck out of this place right now or I'll smash your head in with this two-by-four.' They were scared of whatever I represented. I instantly realized what it was like to be hated for how you look. When I got outside, it really hit me like a ton of bricks," recalls Fairbairn.

Our agent booked us into a cadet hall in Terrace, BC. We showed up the night before the gig and thought we'd drop off our gear, then find a place to stay. We knocked on the back door, and this old guy comes out. I told him we were the band booked to play the next evening. The guy looks us up and down and says, "Nobody's booked this hall—not for you guys." I pulled out the paper I had with the name, address, and other information about the gig, and I asked him, 'Isn't this the place?" He says, 'Yeah, but tomorrow it's a guy who's booked a lapidary show, you know, gemstones and minerals. I thought to myself, *lapidary show?* Then I realized he'd agreed to book the hall for a "rock show." I told him, "This isn't about rocks—this is a rock band!" He panicked, and said, "Oh, no. About a year ago I booked a rock band here, and they trashed the place. I'm not having rock bands here. Get the fuck off of my property!"

Despite problems touring outside the city, the Ambleside Blues Band always loved the homecoming shows they played at the Commodore and their hometown contingent of North Vancouver fans. "Drew Burns was fair and square, a great guy," says Fairbairn. "We never had any problems at the Commodore with anybody telling us to turn it down or dress differently. It was a fantastic place to play."

Ambleside Blues Band, early 1970s,
Luther Fairbairn, far right. Photo:
Courtesy of Luther Fairbairn; poster:
Courtesy of Neptoon Records Archives

Eli

is back in town

with
ALEXIS
AMBLESIDE BAND
NORTH WEST CO.

870 Granville, at the

Commodope

Thursday Aug. 30   2.00
Friday Aug. 31   2.50
ShowTime at 9 p.m.
Tickets at door only !

FULL FACILITIES

tolin

Clockwise from top left:
Commodore calendar, October–
November 1974, Courtesy of
Neptoon Records Archives;
Slade, 1976, Courtesy of Neptoon
Records Archives; Spencer
Davis Group, 1974, Courtesy of
Neptoon Records Archives

And while Vancouver bands might have sometimes encountered difficulties playing out of town, other musicians travelled from afar to play and reside in the city. Born in the musical hotbed of St. Louis, Missouri, Jim Byrnes was exposed to blues and early rock music on the radio and at blues clubs where, as a teenager, he and a friend were often the only young faces in the audience. After studying acting at Boston University and drawing a tour of duty in Vietnam, Byrnes moved to Vancouver in 1971, working odd jobs and playing music. In 1972, when he was twenty-three years old, he was hit from behind by a car while helping push a friend's stalled truck on a highway. Byrnes lost both of his legs.

"The first time I ever went to the Commodore was for the Captain Beefheart show," Byrnes recalls. "I was coming out of a year-long haze from my accident when I went. I loved the slide guitar, and [Beefheart] had such a good band. It was one of those nights you remember and don't remember, if you know what I mean. The audience was howling at the moon that night. That was back in the day when people were into howling at the moon more," he laughs.

In the wake of his accident, Byrnes began to pursue music with more focus, and within two years he would be performing regularly at the Commodore himself, opening for the Goose Creek Symphony on New Year's Eve of 1975. It was the start of an acclaimed career as one of Canada's best blues musicians and the recipient of multiple Maple Blues and Juno Awards. Over the years, he's shared the Commodore stage with a who's who of blues legends. He fondly remembers performers he got to know there, such as Papa John Creach, for whom he opened in 1979. "He was getting on [Creach was born in 1917], but he

Jim Byrnes at the Commodore, mid-1970s.
Photo: Dee Lippingwell

"Muddy Waters [shown here in 1980] could really hold court backstage," recalls Jim Byrnes. "He was the emperor of all he surveyed." Photo: Courtesy of Charles Campbell

certainly knew how to put on a show," says Byrnes. "He was a maniac onstage, but a really sweet guy. Those old guys are like that—they came up the hard way. He was happy that young people were checking him and his music out. The warmth of his personality came through in the music, but hanging out with him backstage was fantastic."

In 1987, Byrnes opened for "master of the Telecaster" Albert Collins at the Commodore. "We had mutual friends and were able to bond," Byrnes says. Collins, who passed away in 1993, is remembered for his irreverent stage performances, frequently leaving the stage while still playing to mingle with the audience. With the use of an extended guitar lead, he once left the club where he was playing and walked up the sidewalk to the store next door to buy a candy bar—without once stopping his act. "Albert had a fantastic sense of humour," Byrnes recalls. "He was another of one of these guys who were great stars in my mind, but didn't act like stars were supposed to act; he was just like one of the guys you'd meet down at a barbershop and chat with. He dug what we were doing too … He gave us some respect, which was so nice for me, a middle-class white kid playing blues music—he got that I understood what it was about. To get support from somebody like him was tremendous."

Byrnes also recalls that in 1981, blues legend Muddy Waters came to the Commodore.

I'd opened for him a number of times over the years in different places and knew him a bit, so I was going to go down and say hi and catch the show. But that same night, Paul Mercs was putting the Charley Pride show on early [in the evening], down at the Orpheum [Theatre]. Muddy was on late at the Commodore. So after his show, I brought Charley over to the Commodore and took him backstage to meet Muddy. Now, Charley and Muddy were obviously from different musical scenes, but they were born about two hours away from one another in Mississippi.

When we got there, Muddy was sitting in the dressing room with a bottle of champagne, wearing a suit and silk socks—he could really hold court, he was the emperor of all he surveyed. When I came in with Charley, they were both kind of gobsmacked. The first thing that Muddy says was, "Man, you know I love that song about going to San Antonio." They were fans of one another, but they'd never met before. They talked a little bit of business, but then they got into what was really big for them, which was baseball. Muddy had been a pretty good country baseball player, and Pride had pitched for the minor leagues' Memphis Redbirds in the early 1950s. Sitting backstage at the Commodore Ballroom with Muddy Waters and Charley Pride, listening to those two guys talk about baseball is one of my favourite backstage memories.

In the 1980s, when Byrnes needed a new pair of prosthetic limbs (the cost wasn't entirely covered by provincial medical insurance), a fundraiser was organized at the Commodore. "Billy Cowsill, Powder Blues, Bolera Lava, and a bunch others all played that night, " says Byrnes. "Drew [Burns] gave us the door, and I was able to get the upgrade I needed … Vancouver, man, the way people rallied around me here with a night like that and helped me when I was really down years ago, when

THE COMMODORE BALLROOM
PRESENTS

JAMES COTTON
SATURDAY, FEB. 5TH

DOORS: 8:30 P.M. SHOWTIME: 9:15 P.M.

TKTS: AT ALL VTC/CBO OUTLETS, INFO CENTRES,
WOODWARD'S, EATONS AND A & B SOUND (DOWNTOWN)
PHONE CHARGES: 687-1818 INFO: 687-4444

THE COMMODORE BALLROOM
PRESENTS

BUDDY GUY
AND
JUNIOR WELLS
"Chicago Blues and Soul"

Special Guest Artists
The Wailin' Demons
featuring...
Jack Lavin & Al Walker

Friday September 20th
Saturday September 21st
Doors 8:30 PM

Tickets VTC/CBO and all usual outlets.
Plus Zulu, Revolutions and Black Swan Records.
Info 280-4411 • Charge by Phone 280-4444

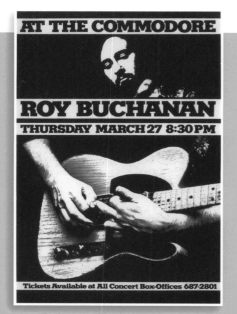

AT THE COMMODORE
ROY BUCHANAN
THURSDAY MARCH 27 8:30 PM

Tickets Available at All Concert Box-Offices 687-2801

Clockwise from top left: James Cotton, 1983, Courtesy of Neptoon Records Archives; Buddy Guy and Junior Wells, 1985, Courtesy of Neptoon Records Archives; Roy Buchanan, 1975, Courtesy of Neptoon Records Archives; Junior Wells and Buddy Guy at the Commodore in 1987, Photo: Charles Campbell; Commander Cody was paid $500 for his February 1977 show, letter Courtesy of Neptoon Records Archives

MAGNA ARTISTS CORP.
9200 Sunset Blvd. Los Angeles, Ca. 90069
(213) 273-3177

February 1, 1977

Mr. Drew Burns
870 Granville
Vancouver, B.C. V621k3

RE: NEW COMMANDER CODY BAND
February 27, 1977

Dear Drew;

Please find enclosed five (5) copies of the contract covering the abovementioned engagement.

Please sign all copies and return them along with the required deposit to my office no later than February 10, 1977. A fully executed copy will be forwarded to you as soon as possible.

Sincerely,

MAGNA ARTISTS CORP.

STAN GOLDSTEIN

/djc
encl.

I had nothing—people accepted me and gave me a chance to play and gave me a break here and there. I owe this city and I'm still trying to pay it back."

The list of bands and musicians who performed at the Commodore throughout 1976 and 1977 in particular is a who's who of blues and country artists, including James Cotton, Charlie Musselwhite, Earl Scruggs, Jerry Jeff Walker, and Vassar Clements. The Commodore's past was also acknowledged when Burns continued to bring in big band acts that were still on the road, such as the Buddy Rich Orchestra, the Duke Ellington Orchestra (led by Duke's son, Mercer Ellington), as well as a touring revival of the Glenn Miller Orchestra. In the mid-1970s, local bands like the Ambleside Blues Band, the Cement City Cowboys, Brain Damage, Chilliwack, and Pied Pumkin filled the room between double bookings of big touring acts as diverse as Commander Cody, John Mayall, Taj Mahal, Junior Wells, Buddy Guy, and Peter Frampton. If the Commodore wasn't yet considered a legendary venue, it was about to be.

As the decade came to a close, while the popularity of blues and folk music didn't wane, there was a growing appetite for new sounds, and the local scene would soon flourish like never before. This new music might have passed Vancouver by had it not been for a handful of people who came together just then, at the right time and place. And while punk and new wave would pay little homage to what it considered the dinosaurs of rock, in Vancouver a new concert business grew from its founders' connections with groups like Pink Floyd and Queen.

31 "21 Steps Lead to Nostalgia," *Vancouver Sun*, October 12, 1973.

32 Potter, Greg. "Commodore Celebrates 75 Years of Live Music," *Georgia Straight*, December 2, 2004.

33 "Commodore Ballroom & Beefheart: Never Too Violent," *Georgia Straight*, March 8-15, 1973, 18.

34 Read, Jeani. "Dolls Sang Trash, That About Says It," *Vancouver Province*, March 14, 1974, 16.

35 Stanley, Don. "When You're All Trash, Darling, You've Got Image," *Vancouver Sun,* March 14, 1974, 25.

36 Mackie, John. "New York Dolls Bring Their Glam And Grit Preview," *Vancouver Sun*, February 29, 2008.

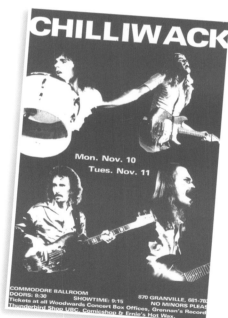

Chilliwack in 1975. Photo: Courtesy of Neptoon Records Archives

{ Brian "Wimpy" Roy Goble of the Subhumans, 1982.
Photo: Lois Klingbeil }

Eight

UP PERRYSCOPE

THE SUMMER OF 1977 was a pivotal period in the cultural landscape of Vancouver. New sounds, familiar to Vancouverites today, were heard for the very first time, including the first blast of the ship's horn on the maiden sailing of the Seabus passenger ferry in Burrard Inlet, and the first whistle of the Gastown Steam Clock. Other sounds, also new to Vancouver, ensured that the city would never be the same again.

On July 30, 1977, Vancouver experienced its first punk rock show. Local band the Furies headlined at the Japanese Hall on Alexander Street with an opening set by the all-female punk band from Victoria, BC, the Dishrags. There wasn't exactly a deluge of media that descended on the show to report on the event or offer any hints that the inauspicious setting was witness to how the winds were changing in rock music. The few local music writers who attended showed up late, most having chosen instead to attend the Journey concert at the Pacific Coliseum, with Emerson, Lake & Palmer opening. The Furies' show went largely unnoticed except by the Hall's neighbours and nearby late-shift railway workers, who couldn't help but overhear the racket on Alexander Street that evening.

Above and right: The Vancouver debut
of the Ramones at the Commodore,
August 1977. Photos: Dee Lippingwell

One week later, at the Commodore on Granville Street, a bigger audience was on hand. It was a night that, in retrospect, seemed to herald a changing of the guard. That evening, four New Yorkers staying at the Castle Hotel grabbed their leather jackets and left the hotel to walk one block to meet the 600 punk rock fans and curiosity seekers who awaited them at the Ballroom. It was the Vancouver debut of the Ramones.

With no larger promoter willing to take a risk on a punk rock show, the concert had been put together and sponsored by *Twisted*, a punk rock magazine based in Seattle published by Robert Bennett, who had also put on a Ramones show there.

The *Georgia Straight*'s music reviewer, Tom Harrison, noted that many of the people who most wanted to attend the show were underaged (the Commodore had a nineteen-years-and-over age restriction) and couldn't get in. So for those who weren't there, Harrison captured how the band had appeared: "Joey is the most unlikely singing idol you've ever seen. Tall! That boy is really tall. Legs as skinny as guitar necks. Rotten posture. He needs those glasses he wears too. Replace those tattered jeans with perma press slacks, his leather jacket with a smock and cut his hair, he'd look just like one of those misfit eggheads who hover slack-jawed over a chemistry set."[37] But Harrison found the night electric, and likely echoed the sentiments of many in the room, writing, "It was a real charge to be thrilled again by four nerds whipping the bangs out of their eyes and giving their all in two-minute packages of concentrated energy."

Harrison also noted the reception given to the band by the Commodore staff. "The bemused executive branch leaned up against a wall and stayed out of the way. The bar crew,

The Pointed Sticks, 1979.
Photo: Lois Klingbeil.

which is into Waylon [Jennings] T-shirts and exchanging jokes with Hoyt Axton and dreaming about Panama Red, looked positively gloomy. Who were these people, masks and pinned together clothes? Crazy mixed up over-nineteen-year-old kids? Who knows? Who cares?"

For the Vancouver audience, this exposure to a live punk rock band was a benchmark and catalyst for the local music scene. In attendance that evening were a considerable number of music fans and local rockers who would quickly cut their hair, ditch any clothes that had hippie overtones, and buy themselves leather jackets—and subsequently go on to form the first wave of Vancouver punk rock bands. Harrison's review reflected just how fresh the punk scene was in 1977: "What the Ramones and bands that have followed in their wake have wrought hasn't been determined yet. It's far too early to tell just how significant punk rock will be culturally, musically, and sociologically years hence." If any omen was needed that rock 'n' roll music was ready for a shake-up and times were changing, a week later Elvis Presley was found dead.

It took another year for Vancouver audiences to absorb what was happening, but there was no turning back. The scene began to build at smaller local venues like the Windmill and the Smilin' Buddha, and a year later, punk returned to the Commodore when the Talking Heads made their Vancouver debut there, followed within a month by "battle-of-the-band" appearances by locals the Subhumans and the Pointed Sticks; the local punk and new wave scene was building quickly.

To audiences, the concert promoter, named at the bottom of the poster or ticket stub, is probably the least apparent part of a concert experience, although they are largely responsible for the show happening in the first place. Ticket buyers come for the bands and will notice the light show, the sound, and even the drum tech before they take notice of the promoter. But within a few short years, music fans in Vancouver would be aware of Perryscope Concerts, and the company's early connection to the Commodore is vital to understanding how the next phase of the Commodore developed.

In 1977, Norman Perry, then twenty-three, and Riley O'Connor, twenty-six, arrived in Vancouver. Both had considerable résumés in the concert business. Originally from Montreal, Perry had worked as a stage manager for the city's legendary concert promoter Donald K. Donald at the Montreal Forum where he "got to see some pretty extraordinary music" from the side of the stage, including bands like Black Sabbath, Jethro Tull, and Led Zeppelin. At nineteen, he moved to England and landed a job with one of the top UK promoters, John Smith Entertainment. These were still the pioneering days of the concert industry, when a young, capable go-getter could rise quickly through the ranks, and soon Perry was handling Rolling Stones tours as an "advance man," making sure the band could stage their increasingly large shows in venues around the United Kingdom.

O'Connor had also left Montreal to travel "on the hippie trail through Europe." In England, he found work for a concert lighting company called ESP Lighting, and rapidly became one of their chief electricians, doing numerous tours with Queen, the Who, Elton John, and ABBA throughout the United Kingdom.

By 1977, Perry had begun to work for Pink Floyd on the upcoming Dark Side of the Moon Canadian tour, determining

Above: Riley O'Connor. Photo: Live Nation Concerts Canada

Left: Norman Perry in 2014. Courtesy Perryscope Produtions US

whether the country's hockey arenas were capable of putting on the shows the band had already done in the UK, when he received a call from Donald K. Donald and fellow Montreal promoter Michael Cohl. Once rivals, Donald and Cohl decided it would be easier (and more profitable) to work together as partners, joining together to expand their concert promotion businesses.

"They had been promoting national tours like Rush and Nazareth," says Perry, "but felt that, in order to properly serve the bands, they ought to set up an office in Vancouver. They'd begun to realize the potential of the whole province and western Canada and wanted boots on the ground there, so they asked if I'd be interested in running it for them. I told them that I'd be coming over to Canada on the Pink Floyd tour, and I'd meet with them to talk about it when I got to Montreal."

By the time he got to Montreal, Perry had thought about it enough, and arrived with a plan of his own. "The first thing I said when I walked into their office was, 'I've decided to move to Vancouver and run a business. Would you like to be my partners?' in my cheeky twenty-three-year-old way," Perry laughs. But Donald and Cohl got on board, and with that, Perry's first call was to Riley O'Connor, as the two had discussed starting a company before. "I had a great job and a good life in England," O'Connor recalls. "To give it all up and start from scratch in Vancouver was a little daunting, but I decided to jump into it." Arriving in Vancouver in that summer of 1977, Perry and O'Connor had ideas in mind for their new venture; both were familiar with how San Francisco concert promoter Bill Graham had built up a diversified, artist-friendly, progressive concert company that presented shows at the city's

Fillmore West, and they hoped to use Graham's model for Perryscope.

Investors Donald and Cohl weren't sure how well Perryscope was going to do, although they felt sure that the two young men had enough connections with American agents to help the new company stay solvent. But Perry quickly realized the kinds of hurdles they faced as the new promoters in town. "It was very much a loyalty business—it still is now," he says. "Traditionally, if you book the act first, you get the first call when they are coming back to town, as long as you haven't done a bad job. Although I had been a promoter in England for many of the bands that could sell out shows in Vancouver, by the time we got to town, thanks to the loyalty system, we weren't going to get those bands."

To stay afloat, Perryscope initially relied on many of the contacts provided by Donald and Cohl, producing Vancouver concerts and western Canadian tours by Rush, Supertramp, and Nazareth. It wasn't an easy transition from the top-tier groups they'd been touring with overseas. "It took me over a year before I stopped thinking I'd made the biggest mistake of my life," O'Connor recalls. "I remember being in Prince Rupert with the Stampeders and telling a guy, 'I could be in Berlin tonight with Bowie.' But I didn't second-guess stuff. I never went back. I figured, now I have to make this work."[38] Perry and O'Connor began to focus on being Vancouver-based promoters.

"John Bauer Concerts, who was bringing shows to town, was [based] in Seattle, and Paul Mercs had moved there too," O'Connor recalls. "Bill Graham had shows coming to Vancouver, but none of these promoters were living there.

[Canadian music band manager] Bruce Allen had Craig McDowell handling his shows in Vancouver—and I mean no disrespect to Craig, because he was there first—but we were the first truly Vancouver-based promoter." Perryscope "lobbied for bands not just when they became hits, but for the emerging acts too," he says. "We had to start from scratch with some of the same people I had cut my teeth with when I started in England. Many of the guys who were junior agents or managers slowly became powerful and in time became the representatives of the next crop of bands."

What had emboldened both Perry and O'Connor to move to Vancouver and start Perryscope was that they considered the city—perhaps more than anywhere else in Canada—ready to embrace the new trends in music. "By the time I left the UK, the punk scene was already well established there. I had seen the early punk rock bands there," O'Connor says.

> But [punk] was pretty unknown in Vancouver or anywhere in western Canada. I knew there was a sort of punk, non-conformist attitude and element in Vancouver that wasn't being tapped into at all. I thought people were tired of the same old shit and the same old people that controlled everything from FM radio to the record companies. So we decided we were going to be street-level guys and work with the import record stores and have credibility at that level. If business and big tours came our way from other, bigger connections we had, that was great, but that street thing was where our heart and blood was, and it allowed us to get our creative juices going and be real promoters. It was an inspiring time.

Perry adds, "I was very fortunate to connect with younger agents who were concentrating on some of the UK acts, like Wayne Forte and the late Ian Copeland…They represented the Clash, the Police, U2, XTC, and more. We were able, with the help of the record companies, to slowly convince these acts that if they came to western Canada they would sell more records than if they toured just in Toronto and Montreal." In 1977, Perryscope set up shop in an office on the ninth floor of Vancouver's historic Dominion Building. "It took awhile for anybody to believe that we were for real," says O'Connor. "We probably came across to some people in the business as a couple of fourteen-year-olds who didn't have any credibility. But we stuck with it."

With the contacts they had, particularly with the new British music scene, Perry and O'Connor envisioned producing a regular concert series to introduce bands to Canadian audiences with affordable "get acquainted" ticket prices. They would use these concerts to build something that the city's music scene had never seen before, making Vancouver an anchor date for touring acts. All they needed was the right venue.

....

37 "Gabba Gabba hey … We're da Ramones," *Georgia Straight*, Aug 11–18, 1977, 20.

38 Buckner, Dianne. "Small Business Tips from Riley O'Connor, Chair of Ticket Giant Live Nation," CBC News/Business, June 1, 2012.

{ Sammy Hagar, 1978.
Photo: Courtesy of Tim Tilton }

CHEAP THRILLS

Nine

As YOUNG PROMOTERS new to the city, Perryscope had a limited number of venues in which to present its concert series. The bands available to them were considered risky—largely unknown to local audiences—and bigger venues like the Orpheum, Queen Elizabeth Theatre, or PNE Gardens were not easily filled and began to be costly the moment the doors opened and the lights were turned on. "The only place we could do these kinds of shows was where the rent wasn't through the roof," Perry says. "If you went to union buildings, you needed a good amount of money as deposit for the rent, ushers, ticket takers, and stagehands, and you needed to bring in a large sound system. You needed an established act to pull all that off."

Perry and O'Connor were aware of the blues, folk, and country acts that were making regular appearances at the Commodore since Drew Burns took ownership. The Ballroom seemed like a worthy candidate—and for O'Connor, it was a venue of choice for additional reasons. "My mother and grandmother, who had lived in Vancouver, told me about going dancing at the Commodore in the 1940s and '50s to big

band orchestras and all these amazing stories about times they'd had there as young adults."

Just as Paul Mercs had, Perry and O'Connor found a receptive ear in Drew Burns. While punk rock and new wave bands might not have been Burns' own cup of tea, he gave them a chance. "Drew basically said, 'If you guys take the risk at the door, I'll take the profits at the bar. Just give me a little bit of money for the door staff and cleanup.' With that, he allowed us to bring in the acts on a much, much, lower break-even—which gave us incentive to go after more acts. We used the Commodore as a catalyst and springboard for all the bands that Riley and I knew from England. And that's how Cheap Thrills began."

The Cheap Thrills concert series inaugural show on January 19, 1978 featured a not particularly avant-garde musical choice—singer/guitarist Sammy Hagar, who'd left the band Montrose three years earlier and was practically an unknown entity on his own. But Perryscope was not going to play favourites in terms of musical genres; they simply presented good music and acts they could believe in.

The reviews of the first show were favourable. The University of BC's student newspaper reviewer, George Huey, observed that after Hagar and the band took the stage, "It didn't take too long for the Commodore crowd to express their appreciation for Hagar's bombastic style. Hagar is about as subtle as a rhinoceros blundering into an afternoon tea social. Yet, despite his exuberance, [he] has enough discipline to put on a good performance." But Huey also noted that "Cheap Thrills is a highly commendable enterprise because all parties involved end up winners. In addition to the low concert prices, the artists are given the exposures they need to acquire a sizeable following. The promoters themselves emerge as heroes who bring high-quality musical acts to town at affordable prices."[39]

In the wake of their initial success, Perry and O'Connor began to assemble a team. Bud Wandrei was just a fifteen-year-old rock 'n' roll music fan in 1976 when he attended a Heart show at UBC; after the concert, he stayed around to watch the band loading out. When student volunteers failed to show up to help, Wandrei and his friends jumped in and gave Heart's crew a hand.

Wandrei, with a pool of high school friends, soon had a burgeoning small business supplying stagehands to local concerts. One day at the Commodore, after he had finished loading some gear into the venue, he struck up a conversation with Drew Burns, who recommended that he connect with Perryscope Concerts for some extra work. "I go over to the Perryscope office, walk in, and right in my face is Riley O'Connor asking, 'What are you doing here!?'" laughs Wandrei. "I was totally intimidated; I was just fifteen years old! But I dropped off my number and told them that if they ever needed help moving gear to give me a call. I never heard anything back, and sort of thought it was a dead end." But a few months later, he got a phone call early one morning. "'Hey, are you still doing stagehand work?' Riley asks me. 'Sure,' I said. 'Okay, we need you.' 'No problem,' I say. 'When?' 'Now! Come down to the Commodore right now!'"

Wandrei called his roustabout friends together, and "we all screamed down to the Commodore. It was a Max Webster and Ian Thomas show that began to load in at ten a.m. I guess

Tom Petty and the Heartbreakers, June 15, 1978. Heartbreakers' keyboardist Benmont Tench recalled, "It was a really big deal for us to be able to play the Commodore." Photos: Lois Klingbeil; poster: *Georgia Straight*

Bud Wandrei with Ozzy Osbourne, 2014. Unknown photographer. Bud Wandrei's April Wine pass from 1981.

Riley's usual crew cancelled on him or something, but we were down there all day, and by the time the show was over, got the band's gear loaded back onto their truck, and were wrapped, it was five a.m. Our pay was just thirty-five dollars apiece, but we loved it! We were just kids and happy to be in the middle of it." If it was still possible to run away with the circus in 1978, Bud Wandrei did it. Soon he was working at Perryscope shows regularly and as a crewman for O'Connor, quickly rising through the ranks to become one of their main production managers.

When Wandrei started there, Marion Dillias, whose husband Johnny was one of the Commodore's first proprietors, had been working as the accountant for almost fifty years. In her ledgers, she kept track of the dozens of events and company banquets held at the Ballroom. "You'd hear her voice over the in-house pager," Wandrei recalls. "She had a voice like Marge Simpson on acid." He also fondly recalls Drew Burns.

Everybody loved him. He got to work at the Commodore, in his baby-blue Lincoln Continental, before anyone else. He was a smoker then who liked a rum and coke. But he was a polished, really classy guy. His door was always open to guys like me to hang out and bullshit after the show. It was a much more informal atmosphere at concerts then. At the end of the night, once the gear had been loaded out, if a band or even some staff wanted to sit around, play cards, have a few drinks, or shoot the shit, he'd stick around too. I think his favourite thing was not so much the shows but the relationships he had with the musicians as people.

Before much of the business was done, as it is today, over impersonal email, both bands and agents had a more direct connection with the promoters and club managers who looked each other in the eye and shook hands on deals. "There was a lot of loyalty back then, and relationships were really important to everybody," continues Wandrei. "Like when Tina Turner would arrive [at the Commodore], she'd seek Drew out to say hello, first thing."

> Back then, the band would come into the building, and you'd all just hang around together. There wasn't really the separation between bands, tour managers, stagehands, club owners, and bartenders like there is now. I remember that, before a Talking Heads show, a young lady came up to me and asked me if we knew where she could get some pot. I said, "Sure, no problem. Is that all you need?" Well, I then realized she was Tina Weymouth, the Talking Heads bassist. One of my buddies had some, and after we finished our work, she invited us to her dressing room, and we ended up smoking dope with her before the show. It was all very informal.

Wandrei has countless stories of Perryscope shows he worked during his tenure at the Commodore between 1978 and 1985, and he was privy to some things the audience never saw, like the time he walked into the dressing room to see a topless Tanya Tucker. Another time, Wandrei remembers "watching Joe Cocker on a three-nighter at the Commodore in 1981. He was singing his ass off and drinking vodka straight out of the bottle, like a madman. At one point, he comes off stage—the

The Talking Heads, September 7, 1978. Photos: Ron Obvious Vermeulen

The oddest double-bill in the Commodore's history was when actor Art Carney, playing solo piano, opened for country singer Tanya Tucker in 1979. "He was playing really nice classical music—no one knew he was such a good pianist!" recalls Bud Wandrei. "But for the first few songs, guys kept yelling, 'Hey, Norton!' Carney had to stop and tell them he wasn't Norton [in *The Honeymooners* TV show] anymore. It was a surreal night."
Photo: Dee Lippingwell

band is still rocking—he probably gave somebody a high-sign to play a guitar solo. He goes into the backstage toilet and pukes his guts out in the sink. He takes a little rinse, and then he's back onstage and keeps going. He was knocking them dead out front, but you couldn't imagine how he could do it in that state; he was so hammered."

The Patti Smith show in 1978 is remembered for being the first punk show that was sold out at the Commodore, but Wandrei remembers it for different reasons.

> When Patti came off the tour bus, she asked for a couple of towels because she wanted to take a bath. They were living on the tour bus; they didn't even have a hotel. Backstage, there was a little washroom with a toilet and a bathtub. Now, it was not uncommon to see three or four people in there at once some nights—bands, stagehands, fans, or groupies, it didn't matter; there'd be one person cutting up rails of coke, another guy rolling up a bill, somebody else using the toilet, and if you had to pee, then you had to use the tub for that. That tub hadn't been used for a bath in twenty years. Well, I told Patti awkwardly, "Ah, you don't want to take a bath in there," and she says, "Oh, it's okay—I'll rinse it out afterward." She had her mind set on it, and nobody was going to tell her otherwise. It probably still looked better than some of the plumbing in places she'd lived in, in New York.

Wandrei recalls that during his Perryscope years at the Commodore, everyone pitched in to help. In the fledgling company, every employee carried concert posters to put up

Patti Smith backstage pass, 1988.
Courtesy of Tim Tilton

Patti Smith, 1978.
Photo: Dee Lippingwell

and had tickets to drop off at record stores. For Wandrei, the job sometimes took an unexpected turn.

> We had a show with a band called Jules and the Polar Bears, and it was really hurting for ticket sales. So Norman [Perry] gets booked on the entertainment segment for the local TV station CKVU, trying to plug the show. He calls me that day and tells me to come into the office. I go in and see that he's rented a polar bear suit. "What's with this?" I say. "Well, Bud, you're wearing this on TV tonight." So I wear this fucking suit and, under the hot lights, I'm sweating like a pig. But the polar bear stunt got written up in the papers and helped plug the show. That's what we did. Everybody had to pitch in. There were crazy ideas like that all the time.

Even more difficult than wearing a polar bear costume was loading gear into a building that was never designed for the increasingly bigger, heavier sound and light equipment that rock bands brought on tour. "In those years, before the Commodore had a freight elevator, there were only two ways to load in," explains Wandrei. "One was through a little five-foot-wide service elevator—you'd be pushing music gear through the kitchen, past the cooks, out onto the dance floor to the stage. But a lot of this stuff was too big for the kitchen elevator. So if you couldn't fit it in there, you had to carry it up the back fire-exit stairs, all thirty-five steps. You'd have eight guys carting lighting trees or 500-lb stereo boxes by hand up the stairs. Had anyone lost their grip or footing and dropped them, they would have been crushed. It was crazy."

Despite the challenges, Wandrei recalls that Cheap Thrills shows "were great. The tickets were just $2.99 or $3.99. They really got things going and nurtured the bands to new audiences. It's important to remember that, for the most part, this wasn't music that was getting heard on the radio."

Perryscope's early achievements weren't going unnoticed. In 1979, the company was spotlighted in *Billboard* magazine: "In its first calendar year, Perryscope has gone from '0 to 60' in establishing its presence in western Canada and can take credit for the innovations the company has introduced in this area and the courage of several of its concerts."[40] Vaughn Palmer, then the *Vancouver Sun*'s music writer, concurred: "What Norman Perry and the Perryscope people did took guts and determination...It was genuine entrepreneurship, and they risked a lot on acts that nobody knew."

Part of Perryscope's plan to reach music fans in Vancouver had been to connect not only with sympathetic local radio stations, but also with local record stores. Before the Internet, diehard music fans often hung out in record stores all afternoon, debating with store clerks about the best bands, albums, and concerts. The people running these independent shops were generally the most knowledgeable about what was new and interesting or just worth a listen, what bands you needed to hear before they came to town, and what local bands you should have already seen.

Gerry Barad was working at Quintessence Records store on Vancouver's 4th Avenue, near the University of British Columbia, when Norman Perry and Riley O'Connor first came into the store. Barad was one of the underaged teens who'd sneaked into the New York Dolls show at the Commodore four years earlier. He later had his own show on the University

The first time that D.O.A. played the Commodore, for the *Georgia Straight*'s Tenth Anniversary party in 1977, recalls Joe Keithley, "we played about three, four songs, and half the room left 'cause they were all hippies. At that point, the Commodore people freaked out because they were losing bar sales. So Drew wanted to pull the power on us. Paul, the stage manager, was trying to unplug the power cord, and we got on the other end of it and ended up in a shoving match, at which point we were ejected. That was our introduction to the Commodore." Despite this unpromising beginning, D.O.A. has played the Commodore more than twenty times since then. Photo: Bev Davies

of BC campus radio station CiTR, and was connected with the local punk rock scene. Perryscope hired him at the end of 1978, where he "became a jack of all trades and learned a bunch of stuff—ticketing, promotion, lighting, sound, the merch business, marketing—you name it," he recalls.

"Music was stagnant then," Barad continues. "Prog rock was shit, and the Americana stuff was all crap, and all we had, that was our own, was the punk rock or new wave stuff." Quintessence Records was often the only store to stock records by the bands that Perryscope booked. The significance of Quintessence Records as a meeting point and hangout for like-minded musicians and music fans can't be overstated. It was one of the few places in Vancouver to stock imported records and hard-to-find gems unavailable at the average record store. Norman Perry says, "There were other progressive record stores, but Quintessence Records was really special; they were selling fifty percent of the tickets for our shows at their one location alone."

As Perryscope grew, it began to influence the local music scene, in part by giving local bands the opportunity to open for the larger acts coming through town. "Giving bands like D.O.A. or the Pointed Sticks opening slots helped the scene," says Barad. And local audiences were, in turn, regularly exposed to acts they might not otherwise have seen. Perryscope gave great exposure to local bands, and one of the best places to do so was at the Commodore. "There were small clubs and Legions," where local bands could perform, remembers Barad, "but the Commodore was like Mecca."

39 Huey, George. "Hagar Opens Concert Series," *The Ubyssey*, January 27, 1978, 17.

40 Harrison, Tom. "How the West Was Won," *Billboard*, January 27, 1979.

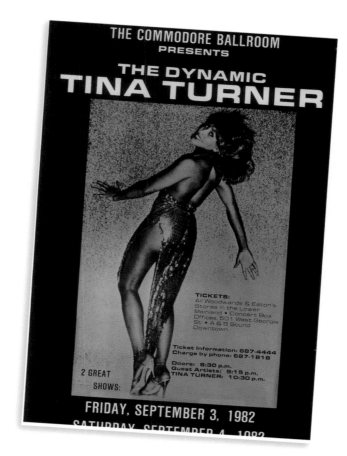

Tina Turner, 1982. Poster: Courtesy of Neptoon Records Archives

{ Debbie Harry of Blondie at the Commodore,
January 2, 1979. Photo: Ron Obvious Vermuelen }

Ten

THE LATE 1970S and early '80s found the Commodore developing into the venerated concert venue it is today, and the Ballroom was busier than ever; Perryscope, other promoters, and Drew Burns himself brought to the stage some of its most legendary performances. It's difficult to single out any one period as the venue's most notable or remarkable, but the month of January 1979 might have that distinction.

It kicked off on January 2, when Blondie made its Vancouver debut. "Picture this," the *Vancouver Sun* reviewer wrote, "a teenage starlet, hair hopelessly blonde, bouncing like a beach ball across the stage of the Commodore … In Europe, they are hot stuff, status that hasn't come in stodgy old North America yet. But Tuesday at the Commodore, Blondie packed the place, another indication of Vancouver's fast growing corps of new wave seekers."[41]

A few days later, on January 6, the Ramones returned to the Ballroom for a sold-out show, with local band D.O.A. opening. "I remember seeing a woman on 4th Avenue who looked punk putting up posters for the show and I talked with her about it," says Grant McDonagh, who's operated Zulu

The Ramones, 1980. Photo: Bev Davies

Records, Vancouver's oldest independent record store, since 1981, but was then a sixteen-year-old high school student. "I went to the show, and it was incredible. I loved them. It was an amazing gig." McDonagh wouldn't let his status as a minor prevent him from missing shows. He used two tactics to get into the Ballroom. "Often, we'd walk in close behind older people, pretending we were with them so the door guys might think we were the same age, and we wouldn't get ID'ed. But if that didn't work, our back-up plan was always to sneak in the back door."

McDonagh's experience of the Ramones show at the Commodore hit him on more than just a musical level. "Back then, Rush poppers had just crossed over from the gay to the punk scene, and you'd see bottles passed around at shows," he says, referring to the recreational inhalant that had been a part of the gay club culture and the early disco scene. "I was right in front of the stage at the Commodore for that show, and some guy next to me shoved a bottle of Rush right under my nose. I'd never done it before. Johnny Ramone was six or seven feet ahead of me playing away as I huffed and the crowd from behind surged hard against us. It was a hell of a moment—standing in front of Johnny blasting the Ramones guitar sound—it was face-melting!"

The Ramones' show looked positively quaint compared to the one on January 12 when Devo made their Vancouver debut, playing both 8:00 p.m. and midnight shows. "It was weird," recalls Stan Heisie, who has regularly attended Commodore shows for more than forty years since seeing Captain Beefheart in 1973. "There was no opening act, but some films that Devo had made were shown on a screen. Everyone sat on the floor

The Ramones, 1979. Photo: Lois Klingbeil

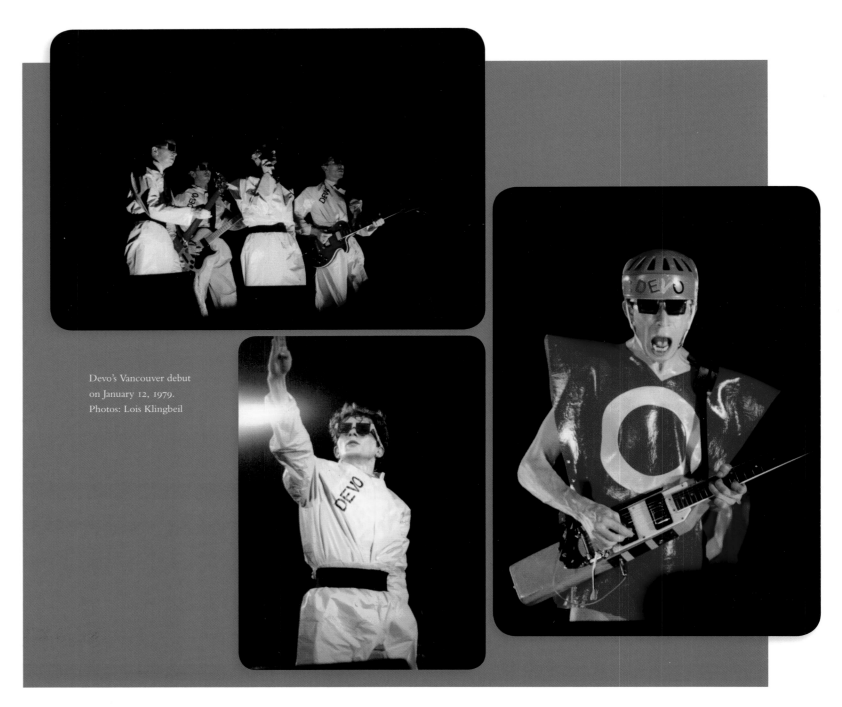

Devo's Vancouver debut
on January 12, 1979.
Photos: Lois Klingbeil

and watched and didn't talk to one another. It was like some statement about the future!"

While Devo may be regarded today as a kitschy '80s group, the band struck audiences as controversial in its early years. *Rolling Stone* magazine notoriously found their sound, imagery, and disdainful "devolutionary" worldview threatening enough to call them fascists.[42] Even the local *Georgia Straight* review noted that Devo "leveled the place ... with calculated irreverence, disciplined theatre, rote precision, and jangling new wave music." The reviewer thought that their cover of the Rolling Stones' "Satisfaction," took "one of the songs most identified with the 60s and an anthem to unrequited sexual passion, and turned it into a mechanical, passionless piece that both deflates the machismo of that whole school of rock and roll while commenting on the mechanical, passionless 70s."[43]

Vaughn Palmer, who currently lives in Victoria where he has covered provincial politics for the last thirty years, was then a music writer for the *Vancouver Sun*. He wrote: "In a little over an hour at the Commodore on Friday night, this marvelous band of loons left 1,100 stunned concert goers with a lot to think about. Their brand of wild, stuttering rock ... is the most motivating music I've heard in awhile and surely the most original debut seen in these parts, and it's nice to hear a hot band with the bit between its teeth."[44]

But Palmer reflects that this was also "a strange time. Music that was incredibly popular and filling arenas was one thing, and then there was this whole new wave punk thing ... Now, twenty-five years later, bands like Talking Heads, Elvis Costello, and the Clash—who all played the Commodore— are the bands that we're still talking about."

The North American debut of the Clash capped off January 1979 at the Commodore. The band had already generated significant hype: When they arrived in Vancouver two days before their show, they did interviews and even held an impromptu pick-up soccer game at McBride Park in Kitsilano against various media, members of local bands, and record store employees. The night before their Commodore show, the band caught a performance by local punk group the Rabid, who played at the Windmill, a small bar at 1047 Granville Street that was, for a few months (before Vancouver's punk rock scene began to congregate at the Smilin' Buddha), the regular punk hangout.

On the afternoon of the Clash show, Riley O'Connor drove out to the airport to pick up Bo Diddley, who, with the Dishrags, opened the bill.

We didn't have a limousine or the money for anything like that, so I went to pick him up. Back then, my car was a green 1972 Ford Galaxy station wagon. Bo Diddley comes out and says, "Is this your car?" "Yeah," I tell him. "Great!" he says. We throw his stuff in the back, hop in, and the goddamn car won't start. I turn to Bo and say, "Listen, I'm sorry, I'm really embarrassed. You deserve better than this. We're just starting off, and we don't have a lot of money." He says, "Don't worry about it, kid. Try to fire it up again." I try it and nothing happens. So Bo gets out of the car and says, "Pop the hood." I open it, and he's in there unscrewing the air filter—one of those old big fat barrels. He lifts the whole thing off, jams his fingers down the carburetor, and yells "Fire it up!" I turn it over, and it starts up! Bo yells, "Now we're good to go!"

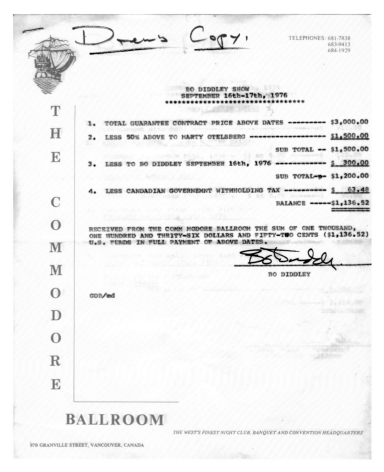

THE COMMODORE

TELEPHONES: 681-7838
683-9413
684-1929

Drew's Copy.

BO DIDDLEY SHOW
SEPTEMBER 16th-17th, 1976
••••••••••••••••••••••••••••••••

1.   TOTAL GUARANTEE CONTRACT PRICE ABOVE DATES --------- $3,000.00

2.   LESS 50% ABOVE TO MARTY OTELSBERG -------------------- $1,500.00
                                          SUB TOTAL -- $1,500.00

3.   LESS TO BO DIDDLEY SEPTEMBER 16th, 1976 ------------- $ 300.00
                                          SUB TOTAL -- $1,200.00

4.   LESS CANDADIAN GOVERNEMNT WITHHOLDING TAX ----------- $ 63.48
                                          BALANCE ------$1,136.52

RECEIVED FROM THE COMM MODORE BALLROOM THE SUM OF ONE THOUSAND,
ONE HUNDRED AND THRITY-SIX DOLLARS AND FIFTY-TWO CENTS ($1,136.52)
U.S. FUNDS IN FULL PAYMENT OF ABOVE DATES.

BO DIDDLEY

GDB/md

BALLROOM

THE WEST'S FINEST NIGHT CLUB, BANQUET AND CONVENTION HEADQUARTERS

870 GRANVILLE STREET, VANCOUVER, CANADA

Signed Bo Diddley contract, 1976.
Courtesy of Neptoon Records Archives

When he gets back in, I ask him, "How the hell did you know all that?" and he says, "Hey—my wife's got the same car!"

While Bo Diddley might have seemed an unlikely support act for the Clash, they wanted to honour the black roots artist and rock 'n' roll legend by having him aboard for the whole tour. Unfortunately, the Vancouver audience, who were more interested in hearing the Clash than the Bo Diddley beat, didn't give him a warm reception that night.

Tim Tilton began at the Commodore in 1975 as a soundman with Kelly Deyong (who supplied the PA to the Ballroom), and was eventually hired by Drew Burns as a stagehand and all-around go-to man at the venue. Perhaps no one has more stories about the Commodore than Tilton, from the night that James Brown refused to perform a second set until someone got him some blow (and once they did, he played until well past 3:00 a.m.) to the night that Def Leppard, after concerts in Morocco and London, performed at the Commodore and set a world record by playing three concerts on three continents in twenty-four hours. But the 1979 Clash show sticks out in Tilton's memory.

"Their lighting guy came in, said hi to us, and let us know they were carrying thirty-three lights they needed to put up," recalls Tilton. "I said, 'Look, we have 100 amps for the whole building. If you're going to put all of those up and keep them on, you're going to blow the power in the building'—and that had already happened twice, with Nazareth and with Doug and the Slugs. The Perryscope guys had to phone the city and get a BC Hydro [electrical utility company] truck to come down and hook an extra powerline tap to the building. I can't imagine what it would cost to try to pull that shit off today— on the afternoon of the show." However, the Commodore must have meant something to the Hydro employees; the club had, for years, hosted BC Hydro staff parties, and Drew Burns also made sure a case of beer ended up in the back of the truck after the workers hooked up more power to the building. The Clash got their light show.

"There was a lot more camaraderie then," explains Riley O'Connor. "People would chip in to help out because it was new and fun and exciting. Today, it's often all business, and you have somebody saying, 'Here's my bill,' but there was none of that then."

As with the nights that Captain Beefheart, the New York Dolls, or KISS played the Commodore, the Clash show is remembered as another you-had-to-be-there, unforgettable night in the ballroom's history. "That night, the dance floor was rocking," remembers Gerry Barad. "The crowd was crazy! But my fondest memory of that night is that the Dishrags, who kicked things off, asked the Clash if they could do a version of their song 'London's Burning,' and the guys in Clash stood by the side of the stage as they played, loving every second of it." At the end of the night, when the Clash came out to perform their encore, they introduced "London's Burning" as a song by the Dishrags.

The packed house that night included a broad mix of people, but Grant McDonagh recalls a kind of borderline between the front and the back of the room. "There was a division between the record company and radio guys in satin baseball jackets and blazers, who'd come to see what the hype

The Clash at the Commodore, January 31, 1979. Photos: Lois Klingbeil

The Clash, January 31, 1979.
Photo: Dee Lippingwell

was about, at the back of the room, and the rock and punk music fans who pushed up to the front of the room to see the band. Back then, the music business people were like the opposite of what you wanted to be."

Nevertheless, from the moment that Clash guitarist Mick Jones stepped on his phase shifter pedal and left it on for the rest of the set and the band roared into "Complete Control" before launching into "Drug Stabbing Time," "I'm So Bored with the USA," and "Tommy Gun," Vancouverites could see for themselves that despite the bombast—the Clash were called "The Only Band That Matters"—they were a terrific live band. John Armstrong (Buck Cherry) of the Modernettes was in the audience that night too. "When you see somebody play live, and you're ten feet away from them, you can tell the ones who were saved in the studio and the ones who are legitimate," he says. "They were a great rock 'n' roll band."

"There was an amazing vibe in the room," recalls O'Connor. "You knew there was something special when they were onstage." Grant McDonagh agrees that it was "a great night," but adds, "I'd seen shows by some of the local bands that were just as good. The local punk scene was already pretty established by then, and there were local bands playing amazing shows all the time. It was an exciting period."

Between Blondie, the Ramones, Devo, and the Clash, which Perryscope brought in that month, plus shows by B.B. King and Tower of Power that Drew Burns booked and promoted, January of 1979 is still remembered as a legendary month at the Commodore. "The Commodore made the world very small," says John Armstrong. "You'd read articles about bands from other places, and then four months later,

they'd be playing in your city. In January 1979, I pretty much blew my welfare cheque on Commodore shows. There was no money left for food."

41 Palmer, Vaughn. "Blondie Wows 'Em," *The Vancouver Express*, January 5, 1979, 18.

42 Goldberg, Michael. "Devo: Sixties Idealists or Nazis and Clowns?" *Rolling Stone*, December 10, 1981.

43 Harrison, Tom. "Q: Are We Not Amused? A: Endlessly!" *Georgia Straight*, January 19–25, 1979, 23.

44 Palmer, Vaughn. "Are These Not Men? Close—They Are Devo," *The Vancouver Express*, January 15, 1979, 6.

B.B. King, March 31, 1983. Photo: Courtesy of Neptoon Records Archives

{ Iggy Pop at the Commodore, 1983.
Photo: Dee Lippingwell }

BALLROOM BLITZ

Eleven

Starting in the late 1970s and through the 1980s, thanks to the shows that Perryscope concerts presented, the jazz and R&B artists that Drew Burns booked, and the acts that emerging concert promoters like Peter McCulloch's Timbre Concerts began to stage at the Commodore, the Ballroom experienced a revival. This era also marked the close of the pioneering days of the concert industry, attracting corporate interest and sponsorship as never before. Those who had staked a claim in its early days enjoyed the great expansion of the business over the next decade.

Groups like the Stranglers, Iggy Pop, Depeche Mode, Joe Jackson, the Pretenders, the New Order, XTC, the Buzzcocks, 999, John Cale, the Cure, King Crimson, the Go-Go's, Graham Parker, Joan Jett and the Blackhearts, Rick Danko, and Paul Butterfield all performed at the Commodore. And it wasn't just the rock 'n' roll bands—soul bands like Sam & Dave, blues bands Taj Mahal or Downchild, Cajun musicians like Clifton Chenier, and reggae stars like Peter Tosh also came to play the Ballroom as part of the burgeoning world music scene.

TAJ MAHAL FRIDAY • MAY 23 8:30 PM

COMMODORE BALLROOM

TIX: VTC/CBO & all its usual outlets. Info & phone 280-4444. Service Charge Extra.

Left to right: Iggy Pop and Gary Numan, 1983. Courtesy of Neptoon Records Archives; XTC, March 1980. Photo: Lois Klingbeil; Summer 1981 poster. Courtesy of Neptoon Records Archives; The Cure, August 1981. Photo: Lois Klingbeil; Joan Jett and the Blackhearts, February 1981. Photo: Lois Klingbeil; John Cale, June 1981. Photos: Lois Klingbeil; Taj Mahal, 1983. Courtesy of Neptoon Records Archives

The Police had their Vancouver debut on May 22, 1979 at the Commodore. After three decades performing in stadiums around the globe, Sting still recalls the venue. "You often remember the smaller places more than the very big ones," he says. Poster: Courtesy of Neptoon Records Archives

"It got to the point where audiences maybe didn't even know who the bands were," says Norman Perry about their early success. "But when people saw it was a Perryscope concert at the Commodore, they remembered that they'd had a great time at a previous Cheap Thrills show or heard that their friends had a good time. People would come just because it was one of our shows—because the bands were so good." A memorable example was the Police concert, with the Specials opening, at the PNE Gardens Auditorium in February 1980, after their debut at the Commodore in May 1979. "The Specials were fantastic," recalls Gerry Barad. "They had the next night off, so we asked them if they wanted to play a Commodore show the following day. We announced that show that night from the PNE stage. It sold out the next afternoon—no posters, no nothing."

Many of the ground-breaking touring bands that played the Commodore in the late 1970s and early '80s made Vancouver their only western-Canadian concert date and Vancouver audiences were, in a sense, spoiled by an array of music—more so than any other city in western Canada. The touring bands also helped to foster the local music scene, particularly when audience members left Commodore shows emboldened enough to form their own rock bands.

By the 1980s, some local bands were being given a chance to play the Commodore themselves. Vancouver's music scene—with bands like the Subhumans, D.O.A., and the Pointed Sticks—benefitted from the city's isolation from both the American and Canadian music industry powerbrokers in Toronto. "Vancouver was a music industry backwater in that era," says John Armstrong. He and his band, the Modernettes,

"The Perryscope era of shows was great," says Dennis Mills, who began to perform there as vocalist and saxophonist with AKA (who opened for Captain Beefheart's return to the Commodore in January 1981), and later with Rhythm Mission and local lounge lizards the Jazzmanian Devils. "Everyone went to the Commodore back then. That's where it was all happening. One night, at a time when I was sort of dating two different women, I ran into one of them at the front of the Ballroom and we talked about going home together that night. I'd had a few vodkas already, and by the time I got to the other end of the room, I was talking to the other woman I was seeing. The first girl saw this, came over, slapped me in the face, and walked away! The second girl asked, 'Who was that?' I acted very surprised and said, 'I don't have a clue. I've never seen her before in my life!' I'm not proud of it, but it's a memory of those funny nights at the Commodore in those days."

Photo: Bev Davies

"We got [to the Commodore] thinking we were headlining, and found out we were opening for D.O.A. instead," recalls Dead Kennedys' singer Jello Biafra of their July 1981 show. "No problem—D.O.A. were our friends, but their fans felt differently. We got the 'Vancouver welcome' of beer cans stomped flat and spun like Frisbees at our heads." Still, Biafra has returned to play the Commodore many times, making appearances as guest vocalist with Nomeansno and Ministry. Photo: Lois Klingbeil

were beginning to play around the city in the late 1970s. "If there were any record label people here, none of them had any signing power. The idea of getting signed to Warner Brothers was just a fantasy—not likely or even possible. We figured there must be some far-away place where supermodels pushed wheelbarrows of cocaine and money or something ridiculous like that happened. But Vancouver managed to sidestep the music industry for a long time, and we were left to ferment in our own juices."

Allen Moy was just twenty-one years old when he went to the 1978 Patti Smith show and "walked away from it thinking, *I can do this.*" Moy would go on to start his own punk rock band as vocalist with Popular Front. Perryscope, always supportive of local bands, booked them for a March 1981 Cheap Thrills concert at the Commodore where they were to open for a relatively unknown Irish band on one of its earliest North American tours. That band was U2.

"At soundcheck, I remember seeing Larry Mullen Jr," says Moy, "and thinking he was a pretty good drummer. I spoke with Bono and Adam briefly backstage. Adam seemed to me to be pretty full of himself because they were headlining the show—and he was even younger than me. It was a full night in there, and we got a really good reception for our set."

When U2 came on, Moy recalls that the band performed "I Will Follow." The song "was the one song anyone knew of theirs, a good song. But when they came back for an encore, they played it again. They were so new they didn't even have enough songs yet to play a full night," Moy remembers. "You can imagine their manager rubbing his hands together in the wings, saying 'Go out and play the single again, boys!'"

Perryscope gave Vancouver's own Modernettes the nod to open for Northern Irish new wave band the Undertones at the Commodore on July 2, 1980. After playing smaller halls and punk clubs in town for a couple of years, the band had a growing reputation. "I remember that this was the first time we had a deli tray," says Modernettes frontman John Armstrong. "Backstage, you could get a beer for a dollar from an old pop machine."

When the Undertones went on, the Modernettes endeavoured, in the time-honoured tradition of the opening band, to steal the beer out of the headliners' empty dressing room. "We didn't go through their jacket pockets or anything like that," Armstrong explains, "but we took all their liquor. Mary [bassist Mary Armstrong, a.k.a. Mary Jo Kopechne] took all of their sandwiches and the salami from their deli tray and put them in her bass guitar case for later."

The Undertones, however, may have had the last laugh. "We took off after the show to some party, got loaded, and then left the cases in the practice space," says Armstrong. "By the time we got back to the space, almost a week later, the deli meat was rotting. It smelled awful and took ages to clean out."

The Modernettes performed at the Commodore with the Undertones in July 1980. Photo: Lois Klingbeil

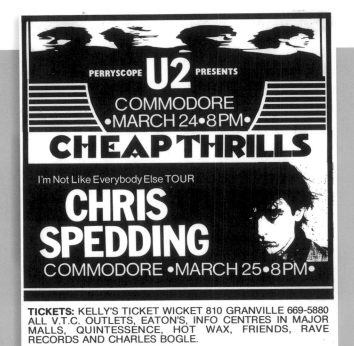

PERRYSCOPE **U2** PRESENTS
COMMODORE
•MARCH 24•8 PM•
CHEAP THRILLS

I'm Not Like Everybody Else TOUR
CHRIS SPEDDING
COMMODORE •MARCH 25•8 PM•

TICKETS: KELLY'S TICKET WICKET 810 GRANVILLE 669-5880
ALL V.T.C. OUTLETS, EATON'S, INFO CENTRES IN MAJOR
MALLS, QUINTESSENCE, HOT WAX, FRIENDS, RAVE
RECORDS AND CHARLES BOGLE.

Perryscope Concerts Present
Echo AND THE Bunnymen
OCT. 26•8:30 PM•COMMODORE

Clockwise from top left: Bono and Adam
Clayton onstage at the Commodore for the
band's Vancouver debut, March 24, 1981. Photo:
Lois Klingbeil; One of Perryscope Concerts
"Cheap Thrills" shows, where tickets were just
$3.99; Echo & The Bunnymen, 1981. Posters:
Courtesy of Neptoon Records Archives

(Managing a rock band is something Moy knows about; after his own band dissolved, he became the manager for 54-40, which he's done for twenty-five years.) But that night, he recalls, he "didn't hear anything remarkable" about U2. "They sounded like some of the other bands of the period. At the time, I personally thought Echo & the Bunnymen were way cooler and seemed to be further along to make the jump to something bigger. I wouldn't have guessed that the band we played with that night would have gone on to be one of the biggest bands in the world."

When U2 returned to Vancouver in 1983, Perryscope worked with them again, this time at the 3,000-seat Queen Elizabeth Theatre. At the time, because rock concerts were banned from playing civic theatres, Perryscope's Riley O'Connor had to make a presentation to the civic theatre board to convince them to let him use the Queen E. After the show, Norman Perry chatted with U2 manager Paul McGuinness. "While the band was having a Guinness and the crew was breaking down the gear, I said to Paul, 'Next time, we'll book U2 at a stadium.' He wasn't so cocky that he agreed with me, but I think he enjoyed hearing that."

U2, of course, is the kind of band that concert promoters hope to discover—the unknown club act of today who goes on to be the theatre or even stadium act of tomorrow. Over the years, when U2 has returned to Vancouver, Bono has regularly mentioned their debut at the Commodore. In October 2009, when the band performed at BC Place, Bono asked the crowd, "Was anybody here the night we first played Vancouver at the Commodore?" The more than 50,000 people in the stadium that night all yelled out, "Yes!"

As U2 grew from being a club-sized to a stadium act, so too did Perryscope flourish. Within a decade of Perry and O'Connor's arrival in Vancouver in 1977, Perryscope had grossed $1.3 million for the U2 show at BC Place, breaking the company's record for a single event. "My last job before coming to Vancouver was as advance man for Pink Floyd. Ten years later, I was their promoter for two sold-out shows at BC Place," says Norman Perry. "So Riley and I went from being just fans to being employees of the band to being their employer. It all happened within ten years," Perry laughs. "It was a dream come true."

By the mid-1980s, O'Connor, Perry, and long-time Perryscope employee Cathy Cleghorn moved to eastern Canada, and a new crop of promoters, Mark Norman and Ian Noble, took over Vancouver's Perryscope office where they continued to promote shows at the Commodore and other venues in the city. "Throughout the '80s there was a big transformation in the music business," explains O'Connor. "The beer companies wanted to be in the game." Labatt bought forty-five percent of CPI, Perryscope partners Donald K. Donald and Michael Cohl's concert company. From these corporate mergers, Perryscope became part of a bigger machine.

O'Connor remained in Toronto, and as a series of buyouts and takeovers made their way through the concert industry, he worked at the helm of Universal Concerts and House of Blues Concerts, which merged into Live Nation, where he is now chairman of Live Nation Concerts Canada. It's a far cry from the early days of Perryscope, as O'Connor has directed the company that leads Canada's live entertainment industry, generating approximately $180 million in annual sales

Various posters from the 1980s.
Courtesy of Neptoon Records Archives

and producing more than 1,100 concerts annually for Canadian and international artists. In 2012, he was inducted into the Canadian Music Industry Hall of Fame. But he still looks back fondly on his years at the Commodore. "We grew up in that place, and I got an education there. It felt like the Commodore became the musical lifeblood of the city, and the concerts we did have a great legacy that I'm very proud of."

Like O'Connor, Gerry Barad also moved on to much bigger positions in the international concert business. Barad left Vancouver in the mid-'80s and currently lives in Chicago where he is now Chief Operating Officer of Live Nation Global Touring, booking tours by U2, Madonna, and some of the biggest artists in the music industry. "Vancouver was amazing then," Barad recalls of his time at the Commodore. "It was a special group of people but also a unique time. I became a promoter at the Commodore, and it helped me get to where I am today."

Bud Wandrei, the teenager who once hung out by the Commodore's loading bay to lend a hand, now works with the Vancouver office of Live Nation Concerts as production manager for some of the company's highest profile concerts at BC Place and Rogers Arena, overseeing shows like Paul McCartney and Roger Waters. "At some of these massive shows today, the guys who work for the bands are often people I worked with twenty-five years ago at the Commodore and other venues. The Commodore was like a high school diploma for me—a real foundation. For a time, it was like a second home. I learned a lot there."

Norman Perry now lives in New York and is President of Perryscope Productions' US office. He continues to work with bands from Pink Floyd to Sting and Paul Simon to Tom Petty. He regards his years in Vancouver and at the Commodore Ballroom as a time when music came of age. "It wasn't the same as when the Beatles arrived or the late '60s wave of bands—that was the ultimate coming-of-age [for rock music]. But I think that time in the late '70s and early '80s was the next great renaissance."

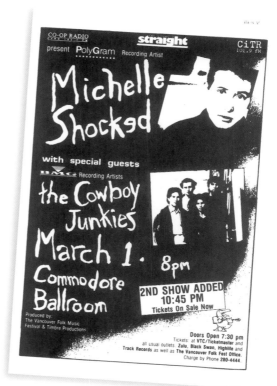

Michelle Shocked, 1989. Photo: Courtesy of Neptoon Records Archives

Vancouver concert photographer Bev Davies captured former
Animals front man Eric Burdon by the Commodore stage door, July
8, 1982. The graffiti had been spray painted months earlier. Burdon
later used the graffiti for a 1988 album title. Photo: Bev Daves

Twelve

BOUNCED

Today, the streets around the Commodore Ballroom are filled with Lululemon-clad joggers clutching designer coffees and running to make yoga class on time. But in the early 1980s, automotive and other industrial shops still lined the streets of the neighbourhood, and more blue-collar workers both worked and lived in this area of Vancouver.

"In a lot of the bars and beer parlours in Vancouver back then, there was a real division between the student drinkers and the working-man labourers," says Vancouver historian Michael Kluckner. "You don't see those people populating Vancouver bars today; you'd have to go up to the interior of the province to find them, because all of that work and industry has moved out of Vancouver." But in the early '80s, that hard-drinking crowd was still a part of the city's bar culture. Taking Trooper's anthem "Raise a Little Hell" as a clarion call on weekends, they would descend on the Commodore, and considered getting into fights part of the evening's entertainment.

Vancouver record store owner Grant McDonagh was in the audience one night at an Undertones concert in 1980

The Commodore Ballroom, 1989.
Photo: Wayne Leidenfrost / Vancouver Sun

when a contingent of boisterous fans and punk rockers were roughly dealt with by venue security.

Halfway through the second song, the band noticed the Commodore bouncers fighting with somebody in the audience and dragging them away. The band stopped the show, and singer Feargal Sharkey shouted out, "We're not going to play if this goes on here!" Well, we thought, *way to go, Feargal*, but it really angered the security, so later they took it out on the audience. When the show ended, the bouncers and friends of the security guards waited for them outside like a gang of thugs and roughed people up on the way out. Some people were hurt, and it got ugly. My friends and I ran out the back door to avoid them. I think that was a real crossroads gig, and in the wake of it, Drew Burns knew that there were certain people who worked there that he had to get rid of.

The Commodore, like most concert venues, needed its own security staff, and when rough crowds often came to the Ballroom, it took a particular kind of person to work as a night-club bouncer. John Jeunesse, known as "Blackie" since high school, grew up in a tough neighbourhood in East Vancouver, but he and his family were originally from Tonga. Attending East Vancouver high schools like Templeton and later Vancouver Technical in the 1980s could be a difficult experience for any teenager, especially one from Polynesia. "There were three kids who used to bug me every day. I said, 'One day, I'm going to smack all of you.' And one day, they pushed all the wrong buttons with me, and I punched all three of them. That's when I got kicked out school altogether." Blackie had a cousin who worked at the Commodore, so he got a job there while still underaged as a dishwasher and busboy. "When I turned nineteen, I got put out front to work as a bartender, but only lasted one night. A big fight broke out in front of the bar, and I jumped over the bar and broke it up really quickly, so [the nightclub management] told me, 'Okay, from now on you're going to work security here.'" Blackie had found his calling.

Well over six feet tall, with a linebacker's frame and hands like oven mitts filled with steak, he is undoubtedly an imposing figure. Yet, as he recalls the years from 1979 to 1995 when he worked at the Commodore, he comes across as quite reserved and unexpectedly good-humoured. (He has since retired from the club security business.) "The first time I saw a big fight at the Commodore was at a Tina Turner show. They didn't have a crowd barricade then. During Turner's show, her top fell off, and all these drunk guys wanted to get up onstage, so a big fight broke out. I had to break it up."

Blackie recalls that the security staff could predict the likelihood of a fight by the type of music that was playing. "Punk rock and blues shows were the worst," he says. Commodore patrons who got too unruly were often ejected from the bar via Commodore Airlines. "It started one night with a drunk who was causing problems. We walked him to the top of the stairs and told him to leave. He turned to yell something back at us and fell from the top of the stairs to the very bottom. He sort of threw himself out! That's when we started calling it Commodore Airlines... Sometimes they fell on their own, but other times we helped them," he says with a restrained smile. "We used to say that the front stairs were first class, but the back stairs were second class because there wasn't a carpet on the back

stairs." Although it seems astonishing today that an establishment would allow security staff to literally throw patrons down the stairs, Drew Burns admitted that this did occur. "We had some big guys on the door. If we had a problem with someone, we'd tell them that they could go out the front way like a gentleman or out the back on Commodore Airlines."

Blackie is well remembered by anyone who worked with him at the Commodore during those years and by Commodore regulars and bands who saw him in action from the vantage point of the stage. "When Blackie was working, you didn't even want to make eye contact with him," says John Armstrong. "He used to scare the shit out of me. I thought that he would have worked there even if they didn't pay him, because it seemed he enjoyed smacking people around so much."

Long-term Commodore stagehand Tim Tilton recalls an incident involving Blackie. "I was backstage after a show and saw Blackie holding Tom Anselmi, the singer for Slow, up against the wall with one arm, saying he was going to kill him. Tom was drunk and had said something wrong to him. Now Blackie liked me, so I tried to calm him down, saying, 'Man, you gotta put him down. He's the singer of the band—you can't choke him.'" Tom Anselmi himself admits that in his younger, drunken days, he didn't always keep his opinion to himself. "I wish I could remember better what I said that set him off," he says. Anselmi and Slow were no strangers to controversy at other concerts as well; organizers pulled the plug during their performance at Expo 86, for example. "That was a pretty volatile show, and I think Blackie felt we weren't suitable for the Commodore. A lot of the staff then, especially the bouncers, were fucked up. It was a rough time there."

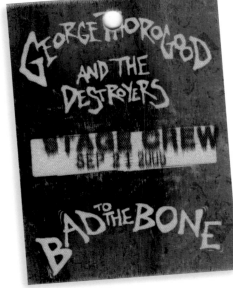

Above: Main bar of
The Commodore,
1980s. Photo: Tim
Tilton

Right: George
Thorogood backstage
pass, 2005. Courtesy
of Tim Tilton

Blue Rodeo singer/guitarist Greg Keelor, recalling when they first began to perform at the club in the late 1980s, says, "The bouncers were nuts there. I remember one night Blackie went on a rampage through the club, tossing people out and punching them." Blackie admits that the Commodore security might have been heavy-handed, but he also stresses that it was not uncalled for, especially when blues-rock acts like George Thorogood and the Destroyers would attract a hard-drinking crowd. "There were a lot of fights at those shows," recalls Thorogood, who was presented with his first gold record at the Commodore. "I remember seeing three fights at once. Sometimes it was scary, and with that dance floor on springs, it added to the craziness." Blackie concedes that on some nights, the fights were out of bounds.

One time, a bunch of guys from Langley came to town, and there was a fight with about ten of them. We kicked them out, but they came back the next weekend with thirty people who wanted to start trouble. We didn't let them in the front door, but a couple of them got in and started to fight. Once we kicked them out, a big fight broke out in front of the Commodore, and it moved up the street, all the way to the next block. When the police finally showed up, they yelled at us for taking the law into our own hands.

However, he notes that times haven't changed entirely for the better. "Now you deal with people who will pull a knife or a gun on you. Most of the time at the Commodore and all the bars, it was just fists. I never saw anybody pull a gun in there. Nobody just fights any more," Blackie says, sounding like a connoisseur of a nostalgic craft lamenting the passing of its golden age.

The nights of ballroom dancing were ancient history, and this period at the Commodore is remembered as an era when some of the city's biker gangs made the place a favoured nightspot. "When some of the Hells Angels started coming to the Commodore, customers were scared of them," Blackie remembers. "They'd show up wearing their colours. But they weren't difficult to handle. I knew some of them from [Vancouver's] East End. Sometimes, if there was a fight between customers, [the Hells Angels would] ask if we needed any help! I always told them—'No, no, we're okay.'"

Commodore stagehand Tim Tilton recalls that Drew Burns didn't like to see the bikers enter the Commodore through the front door. "So there was an arrangement that, if they did show up, they came in the back door, and it was usually just before the band came on. The bikers would park their bikes in the back alley and leave a guy—some junior or hanger-on—to watch the bikes for the whole night. Their leader would stop and say to me, 'Hey, if any of my guys is causing you problems, let me know.'"

But manager Bruce Allen thinks that Drew might have "lost control of the place to the bikers." Although he was not involved with the Commodore in those years, he has a long professional history with the bar and nightclub scene in Vancouver. "Drew is a good guy, but he was content to sit in his office and regale people with stories about the business. I mean, I was one of those people, but bikers were hanging around the Commodore a lot in the '80s."

John Kay backstage pass, 1987.
Courtesy of Tim Tilton

Johnny Winter backstage pass, 1987. Courtesy of Tim Tilton ; Blues acts like Johnny Winter (shown here in 1989) often attracted rowdy, hard-drinking audiences. Winter played the Commodore seven times. Photo: Kevin Statham.

"That was a part of the nightclub back then," recalls Blue Rodeo's Greg Keelor. "I honestly thought there was a meth lab backstage in one room they were always in, with bikers hanging around, doing coke in the bathrooms. It was like something out of a movie."

Blackie recalls a period of time when both police and bikers were at the Commodore, albeit at different times of day. "The bikers often came to shows at night, but during the day, the cops were in the Commodore, looking out the windows onto Granville Street," he says. "The old windows were mirrored, so the cops couldn't be seen. They were doing surveillance and would radio the undercover officers down on the sidewalk, who then arrested the drug dealers."

Discussing the role that the Hells Angels may have played at the Commodore still makes many people who played or worked there uneasy and quick to dismiss the subject. Some say that while the bikers were indeed a regular presence, they were big spenders at the bar who kept to themselves. There are others who anonymously admit to witnessing the bikers walk in and out of the Commodore with bags of money, especially after hours.

If there was a glitch in the nightclub's system that spurred rumours, it was that patrons were required to buy drink tickets in one lineup and then order drinks at the bar in another lineup. On the most innocent level, stories abound that staff members handed out arm-long strips of complimentary drink tickets to patrons with whom they were friendly, and bartenders discreetly gave back drink tickets to good tippers. More seriously, former staff suggest that certain bar managers were raking profits from the sale of drink tickets to put in their own pockets, and Burns was too busy running other aspects of the club to notice. Whether organized crime interfered with the Commodore's business practices or not, most patrons, staff, and musicians at the Commodore in those years found the bikers hard to miss. Krister Kottmeier performed at the Commodore Ballroom in the early 1990s as bassist with local bands Imamu Baraka and the Spirit Merchants, but in 1989, he and future bandmate Steve Dawson, then high school students, sneaked into the Commodore to see legendary blues guitarist Johnny Winter.

A few songs in—and even though it was noisy, we felt and heard a commotion behind us—people started to say, "Watch out, guys, coming through," and everyone made room for a big group of Hells Angels. There must have been fourteen of them. A few didn't have their vests on and just wore supporters' T-shirts, but there was no mistaking them. As everyone got out of the way, the bikers moved up to the front of the stage and watched the show.

Suddenly, a tall thin guy off to the side of us on the dance floor started to honk away on a harmonica, trying to play along with the band. He was drunk and not even playing in the right key. Everyone tried to ignore him, but he was annoying. I saw what seemed to be the head biker look over his shoulder to one of his guys, who then whispered something to another biker standing behind him. That biker walked straight over to the guy playing the harmonica, wound up, and decked him—knocked him flat. Everyone looked stunned but didn't say anything, and the biker casually walked back to his buddies. It was a bizarre,

shocking, and surreal thing to watch, especially for a sixteen-year-old! A few moments later, the bouncers came and dragged the harmonica player off the floor, and the show went on uninterrupted.

Although the bikers were a presence at the Commodore and some of the bouncers may have been heavy-handed, none of this detracted from the quality of the shows. The venue's busiest period was about to begin as the local music scene thrived as never before, with new artists breaking, new clubs opening, and new promoters joining the scene, all of whom found themselves orbiting the Ballroom.

Achin' Blues Balls Band, 1990. Courtesy Neptoon Records Archives

{ Kurt Cobain in the crowd during Nirvana's
March 8, 1991 show at the Commodore.
Photo: Charles Peterson }

Thirteen

NIGHT AFTER NIGHT

The period between the mid-1980s and early 1990s might have been the Commodore Ballroom's busiest ever; it was often open five or six nights a week as Drew Burns filled the calendar with touring acts, local band showcases, charity fundraisers, and university spring-break parties in addition to the annual company parties and banquets that had been a pillar of the Commodore's business since the 1930s. As Burns said, "I used to tell people that when you see nothing happening at the Commodore, it didn't necessarily mean nothing was going on—there was usually a private party happening."

Sometimes the place was busy around the clock. Commodore stagehand Tim Tilton recalls: "Lots of times, Drew would come up to me and say, 'Listen, Timmy, I forgot to mention, we've got an after-grad party coming in here after this show. Can you stay and take care of it?'" Tilton and other staff were left, after working a concert, to keep an eye on a room full of local high school students who sneaked in hip-flasks of alcohol in numbers not seen since the bottle club days.

The Commodore contributed to an explosion of interest

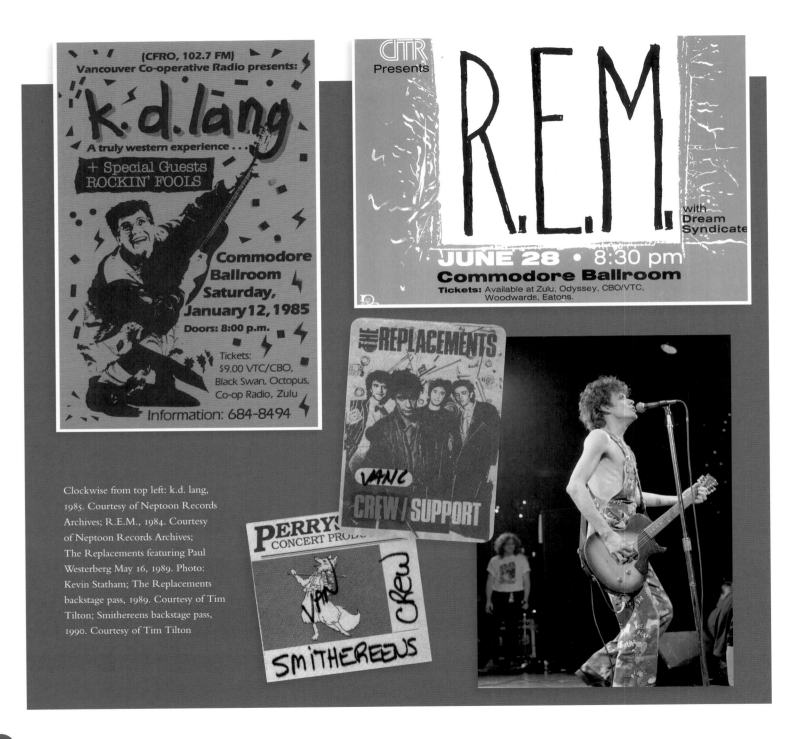

Clockwise from top left: k.d. lang, 1985. Courtesy of Neptoon Records Archives; R.E.M., 1984. Courtesy of Neptoon Records Archives; The Replacements featuring Paul Westerberg May 16, 1989. Photo: Kevin Statham; The Replacements backstage pass, 1989. Courtesy of Tim Tilton; Smithereens backstage pass, 1990. Courtesy of Tim Tilton

in and enthusiasm for live music that generated a steady influx of touring bands from groups as diverse as INXS, Grandmaster Flash, Toots and the Maytals, k.d. lang, Long John Baldry, the Smithereens, the Replacements, Nina Hagen, Roxy Music, Randy Newman, and NRBQ. Up-and-coming local groups and musicians like the Payola$, Images in Vogue, Herald Nix, and Skaboom! also played the Ballroom in this era. New bars opened in the city to support live music, and some old clubs put in small stages and sound systems so they too could bring in live music.

In the 1970s, the Town Pump was a Gastown restaurant that featured a house band playing top-forty hits until Bob Burrows, one of the owners, took over the bookings and started bringing in live music. He noticed that the audience's response was better than it had been for the cover band. The Town Pump became a pivotal live music spot, providing "a venue for an emerging post-punk/new wave community and a wealth of diverse touring acts. It became a stepping-stone for local acts that had graduated from the smaller Railway or Savoy [clubs] and were on their way to the Commodore Ballroom."[45] What developed was a kind of informal circuit within the Vancouver music scene, where both local and touring bands who showed that they could fill a small bar or club could graduate to bigger rooms in the city such as the Commodore.

In the late 1970s and early '80s, while punk and new wave bands were making an impact on the Vancouver music scene with performances at the Commodore, more mainstream acts like the Powder Blues Band and 6 Cylinder also played there. But no group put the Commodore's ballroom dance floor to

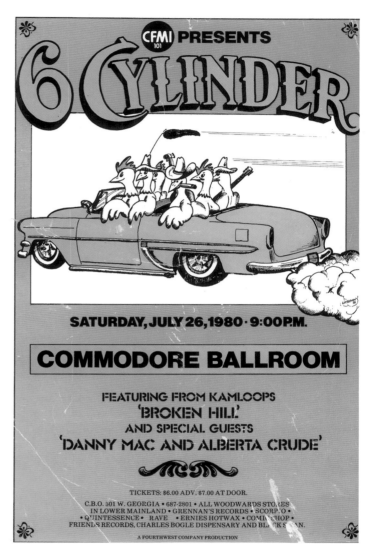

6 Cylinder was a popular local band in the 1980s.
Poster: Courtesy of Neptoon Records Archives

A FOURTHWEST COMPANY PRODUCTION

DOUG and the SLUGS

RETURN FROM RETIREMENT!

THURS. DECEMBER 13 • 1979, 9:00 P.M.

COMMODORE BALLROOM

TICKETS: $6.00 ADV. $7.00 AT DOOR.

C.B.O. 501 W. GEORGIA • 687-2801 • ALL WOODWARDS STORES
IN LOWER MAINLAND • GRENNAN'S RECORDS •
• QUINTESSANCE RECORDS • ERNIES HOTWAX • COMIC SHOP •
FRIENDS RECORDS, CHARLES BOGLE DISPENSARY AND BLACK SWAN.

"The show was a joke retirement gig at the Commodore," explains Doug and the Slugs keyboardist Simon Kendall. "We were making fun of bands that had retired and then done comeback tours. We dressed up as old men and the road crew pushed us out onstage in wheelchairs. As the night went on, we sweated away the 'old man' makeup—it was dreadful!"
Poster: Courtesy of Neptoon Records Archives

use as regularly as Doug and the Slugs, who until recently held the record for most single performances by a band. Doug and the Slugs combined an upbeat, R&B-influenced sound, an infectious sense of humour, and a guaranteed good-time live show that sold out the Ballroom time after time. They performed there as often as five or six times a year, racking up more than forty shows over the course of two decades.

Keyboardist Simon Kendall recalls, however, that it wasn't easy to get their foot in the door. "A lot of clubs wouldn't hire us because of our name," he recalls. "Drew Burns once said, 'No band with a name like Doug and the Slugs will ever play the Commodore.'" Singer Doug Bennett was left to book the band into places like Vancouver's Japanese Hall or Oddfellows Hall—until club owners noticed that the band was attracting crowds and started to book them into their rooms.

"Doug was always trying to make shows special or do something unique," says Kendall. "There used to be a furniture salesman in Vancouver called Harry Hammer, and he would do corny TV commercials where everything was 'nine-ninety-nine!' So we did a show with a special discount ticket of $9.99 and put Harry on the poster, and he introduced the band at the Commodore." One of Kendall's favourite shows at the Ballroom was "one we called The Last Upper—a double bill with us and 6 Cylinder. On the poster, all of us were dressed as the disciples and [Timbre Concerts Promoter] Peter McCulloch was dressed as Jesus."

Although Doug and the Slugs never took themselves too seriously, their singles got significant airplay in Vancouver and charted nationally, scoring a gold record in Canada. They began to tour in the US where, once again, there were issues

Various Doug and the Slugs posters.
Courtesy of Neptoon Records Archives

Bryan Adams at the Commodore, 1980.
Photo: Bruce Adams

with the band's name. "To people in America, a slug was a bullet," explains Kendall, "something to put in your .45—so they didn't get it either."

Doug Bennett passed away in October 2004, and a memorial was held for him at the Commodore, giving family, friends, and fans a chance to say goodbye to the singer who had led what was, essentially, the house band for so many years.

For Kendall, who's performed at the Commodore countless times over the years, not only with Doug and the Slugs but more recently with the Colin James band, the Ballroom has remained a favourite venue. "There's a thing that happens in that room when you get it packed and have a really great band. You can achieve liftoff—you feel like the place is going to levitate—and as a performer, it's one of the most exciting things I've ever experienced," Kendall says. "I saw so many bands there too, and a lot of them were on their way up to the next echelon. Maybe Doug and the Slugs sort of plateaued there. I don't mean to be self-deprecating, but there are worse places to plateau."

One artist who didn't plateau at the Commodore was Bryan Adams, who performed there first in 1980 and again in 1983 before he became an international star. Adams remembers his early performances at the Commodore and notes that these shows came at a pivotal time in his career. "I'd been to the Commodore before and bounced on that floor when I was in the audience," he says, "but to play on that stage was very exciting because the record company came to the show. From that moment, I was a real artist in their eyes. I was no longer someone who just sent in demos; it became tangible."

In 1983, Adams made an important connection with Tina Turner at her Commodore show. Adams' manager Bruce Allen recalls, "We went backstage, and he met her. Bryan was hot then, and Tina wasn't as big in America as she was in Europe. Bryan went on tour with her in Europe, opening for her. He'd come out and do that song ["It's Only Love"] at the end of her shows. It had a hell of a lot to do with him breaking overseas—it was like Tina gave him the official stamp of approval. And that whole thing began one night at the Commodore."

As with Adams, the Commodore would catch many rising performers at the beginning of their careers. Colin James went from being unable to get into the Commodore as a sixteen-year-old to, a few years later, playing a five-night stand at the venue, a record yet to be broken and matched only by Blue Rodeo in 1995. In 1984, James opened for Stevie Ray Vaughan. "I watched Stevie's set from the wings that night, and as a guitar player, it was just punishing [to see] his strength and his ability to stay on it, in the moment. He was so good, it was exhausting," says James.

As often as he played the venue himself, some of his favourite memories are of being in the audience. "Some nights, when I'd finished playing somewhere else, I'd get down there and catch the last few songs by whoever was there. But I'd also run into people I knew there and sometimes end up talking by the bar, or we'd go over to Drew's office where the drinks would flow. He was always great to talk with!" James recalls.

In November 2012, James returned to the Commodore to record a live album to celebrate twenty-five years in the music business. "I'd never done a live record, and it made sense to do it there. I spent a lot of time beforehand trying to decide on the set list," James says. "The Commodore has a real energy.

Clockwise from top left: Colin
James at the Commodore, March
1991. Photos: Kevin Statham;
Colin James backstage pass, 1989.
Courtesy of Tim Tilton; 1988
Colin James poster, Courtesy
of Neptoon Records Archives;
cover of Colin James' 2013 album,
recorded live at the Commodore.

COLIN JAMES
TWENTYFIVE
LIVE

straight and 99.3 FOX present

COLIN JAMES

VIRGIN RECORDING ARTIST
COMING HOME
PARTY with special guests
THE YARD DOGS featuring
LIGHTNING LESTER
THE COMMODORE
Remembrance Day Weekend
NOV. 10
NOV. 11
DOORS 8 PM

Tix: Ticketmaster/VTC and all lower mainland Eaton's & Woodward's Stores. Charge by Phone 280-4444.

Colin James
World
Tour '89
CREW

A venue can dictate what the night is going to be like. So while you can get away with doing a couple of ballads, the Commodore itself wants to rock. That night, we kept things moving, and the energy in that room is contagious, so it was perfect."

The concert business was evolving and new promoters emerged, bringing their own unique musical preferences and interests to the shows they put on at the Commodore. Although the original team had moved on, Perryscope continued to book the room. Drew Burns brought in touring acts and gave local bands, on multi-band bills, a chance to play there on nights when the club would otherwise have been closed. Other independent promoters ensured that Vancouver audiences enjoyed more diversified musical choices than ever before.

Vancouver multicultural outdoor festivals that feature music are now commonplace events that occur every summer, but in the 1980s, when the Vancouver Folk Music Festival was still in its infancy, Mel Warner and his pioneering company Melo Productions began to bring some of the first notable reggae, Latin, and African music concerts into the Commodore Ballroom. Just a few years earlier, that music might have gone unheard without a local champion, but Warner helped to bring world music to Vancouver, and in the process, broadened the musical palate of the city's audiences. Originally from Saint Kitts, he came to Vancouver with his family in 1964. Warner began to work first as a busboy and later as a doorman at Oil Can Harry's. "I used to see [manager] Bruce Allen and [agent] Sam Feldman come in, and I'd hear them wheeling and dealing and listen to them talk about how they went about brokering

Commodore Ballroom advertisement.
Courtesy of Tim Tilton

Ziggy Marley played the Commodore on September 11, 1993; he was one of the world music and reggae acts brought to Vancouver by promoter Mel Warner. Photo: Kevin Statham

deals; I learned some of that business language," he says.

Warner completed a bachelor's degree in science at UBC, but it wasn't until he met Riley O'Connor and the other Perryscope promoters at the Jimmy Cliff and Peter Tosh concert in 1981 at the Kerrisdale Arena that he began to take an interest in the concert business. "They encouraged me to start doing reggae shows. It was like they put something in my drink—the entertainment bug—and it's been in my system ever since," he says. Warner's successful reggae shows in Vancouver in the '80s caught the attention of Drew Burns, who then offered the Ballroom as a venue for Melo Productions.

Throughout the '80s and '90s, the Commodore was home to numerous world music acts, including local reggae bands the Soul Survivors, Small Axe, Fire Temple, and Tropical Breeze. Warner brought in touring acts such as Toots and the Maytals, Burning Spear, Ziggy Marley, and Byron Lee and the Dragonaires. His accomplishments might have been considered less remarkable in another Canadian city like Toronto, which had a larger Caribbean community, but in Vancouver, with a much smaller scene, it's fair to say that Warner is an unsung hero for introducing local audiences to world music groups who might not have made the city a tour stop without his efforts.

The clown prince of Vancouver concert promoters was Bud Luxford, who was raised in North Vancouver. "As soon as I was old enough, I moved downtown. I couldn't take North Vancouver. It was like Surrey with trees," he says with his characteristic sense of humour. Luxford and roommate Nick Jones (from the Pointed Sticks) moved downtown, and the Commodore became almost like a second living room to them.

If Luxford wasn't attending the shows, he was working them. He had been a roadie for Perryscope before he began to work as a merchandise seller at the Commodore, where he was sometimes given additional duties, as when Drew Burns would hand him a megaphone at the end of the night to clear the room once the show was over. "I'd yell at the audience, 'You're no longer paying customers, and you're trespassing. Buy a shirt or get out!' That used to crack Drew up." Luxford and Gerry Barad began to promote shows under the name Pino and Hank Productions. "Those were our nicknames—Pino Rogaletti and Hank Kimble," explains Luxford. "When I was young, I had always wanted to put on a show at the Commodore. So Gerry and I put on a Pointed Sticks show there that sold out. We made even more money than the band! I thought, *I like this*, and that's how I got into it."

In the 1980s, the Vancouver music scene was notable for its prevalence of "fuck bands"—bands made up of musicians from various groups, not playing the instruments they regularly played, and often featuring a ridiculous premise or stage gimmick. The fuck bands usually played covers and did one-off shows. Luxford released a compilation LP of some local fuck bands that was well-received, and in 1981, he decided to do a second album and organized a concert to promote the new compilation.

Budstock '81, held on July 25, 1981, sold out the Commodore. And despite the fact that nobody had ever heard of most of the bands before (and never heard of them again), for many locals, this event still holds the crown for the greatest show of all time at the Commodore. "Budstock had everything—confetti cannons, card girls, naked girls, clowns—we

Bud Luxton staged the infamous
Budstock concerts at the Commodore.
Photo: Bev Davies

Bud Luxford and Gerry Barad brought a spirit
of carnival showmen to the realm of punk shows
at the Ballroom for the Budstock '81 concert;
Budstock '81 card girls. Photos: Bev Davies

used every gimmick we could and every genre of band," recalls Luxford. The lineup included Rude Norton, Buddy Selfish, the Melody Pimps, Mrs. Luxford's Fish, and Jimbo and the Lizard Kings. Gerry Barad himself took a turn as singer in an act called Pino Rogaletti and the IUDs. "It was the greatest show there I ever saw," says Barad. "You could not put that show on in any other city. Those weren't even real bands. We sold out the Commodore Ballroom for five bucks a ticket—a thousand people came to see it!"

Luxford promoted other shows, but not all of them took off. "I booked a show at the Commodore called Christmas It Up one December, and the headliner was a band called Soupboy. It was a piss-take on Loverboy, and all the songs were about soup—"The Soup is Hot Tonight," "Everybody's Working in the Kitchen," and that kind of thing. Ticket sales were lousy for that one, and so I called up Drew. He said, 'Don't worry, it's okay, we can cancel it.' And he didn't take the room deposit. It's too bad we didn't ever get to do Soupboy though," he laughs.

Luxford staged Budstock II at the Commodore on the tenth anniversary of the first event, on July 25, 1991. At a final Budstock III on July 25 1992, a large chair-throwing fight broke out in the audience between Commodore security and a group believed to be either Clark Park gang members or a rival biker group. The evening became notorious in local music history and was dubbed "Bloodstock" by locals. It was notable as well because it included the debut performance of local Celt-punk rockers the Real McKenzies, who still perform and tour worldwide today.

Of all the local independent concert promoters who brought new music to Vancouver, Peter McCulloch's Timbre

Clockwise from top left: Budstock '81 bands included Jimbo and the Lizard Kings, Buddy Selfish, and the Melody Pimps; Budstock handbills. Photos: Bev Davies

Left: David Bowie fronting Tin Machine played the Commodore on December 12, 1991. His set included a cover of the Velvet Underground's "I'm Waiting for the Man." Photo: Kevin Statham

Right: On a rainy November night in 1992, Rolling Stone Ron Wood performed at the Commodore with a backing band that featured Small Faces keyboardist Ian McLagan and regular Rolling Stone backing vocalist Bernard Fowler. Photo: Kevin Statham

Below: Australian bands have appeared regularly over the years, including INXS, Midnight Oil, the Hoodoo Gurus, the Vines, Grinderman, the John Butler Trio, and, as shown here in 1993, Weddings Parties Anything, featuring acclaimed songwriter Mick Thomas. Photo: Kevin Statham

Timbre Concerts, founded by Peter McCulloch in 1981 brought many shows to the Commodore, including the Pixies with Bob Mould in 1989, the Violent Femmes in 1991, Pere Ubu in 1993, and Jesus Lizard in 1994. McCulloch's son and daughter now manage the company. Posters courtesy of Neptoon Records Archives

Clash frontman Joe Strummer filled in on guitar during the Pogues' first appearance at the Commodore in 1987. Local rockabilly band the Nervous Fellas opened the show. "During the day while we were soundchecking," recalls Nervous Fellas vocalist Butch Murphy, "the Pogues were having their dinner at a table in the back. They cheered us on between songs. [Pogues singer] Shane MacGowan talked with me afterward saying he didn't like our band name because he thought we didn't seem nervous at all!" Photos: Kevin Statham

Concerts was responsible for some of the most memorable. McCulloch brought the Pogues to the Commodore in 1987 for a three-night stand. By the late 1980s, the original energy of punk rock was arguably all but dormant, but if it could be found anywhere, it was in the anarchic spirit of the Celtic folk rockers from London. The Pogues' shows at the Ballroom were always legendarily beery affairs that consistently broke bar records, and by the end of the night the entire over-sold room would be singing along in unison to Pogues classics like "A Pair of Brown Eyes" while the band rocked and reeled onstage.

During the Pogues' 1991 tour, former Clash front man Joe Strummer filled in on vocals for beloved and besotted lead singer Shane MacGowan, who had left the band just prior to the tour. In the days before the Commodore show, there was considerable concern about whether the band would be the same without MacGowan. Verne McDonald, the *Georgia Straight*'s reviewer, attended the Commodore show and found that Strummer "has enough whisky-and-snarl in his voice to cover for MacGowan's absence and makes a fine front man for when the band is interested only in making lots of joyous noise… Having announced it was the anniversary of their first gig together, they played like they were out to party, and accordionist James Fearnley leapt around with his squeezebox like a Celtic Pete Townshend."[46]

In a 2014 interview for this book, the Pogues' James Fearnley recalled the show: "I loved the feeling of space and time too, because the ballroom floor—not that I could see much of it because of the crowd—was flanked by columns and receded into the distance. The Vancouver crowd I remember as being particularly warm."

Timbre Concerts brought another famous show to the Commodore in 1991 when Nirvana headlined the Ballroom on October 30 with Mudhoney opening. Billed as "two of Seattle's hottest bands," the show took place a month after the release of Nirvana's breakthrough record *Nevermind*. It was the dawn of a new alternative music scene. Nirvana had, in fact, first appeared at the Commodore earlier that year on a four-band bill, where they stole the show from headlining Screaming Trees.

By the 1990s, the Commodore had earned significance for a whole new generation of musicians in Canada. "The first time we ever played in Vancouver was at the Commodore," recalls Sloan guitarist Jay Ferguson.

We had made a recording in Halifax that got passed around until it caught the ear of a guy at Geffen Records. He said he was going to the Music West festival [in Vancouver] in April of 1992, and that maybe he could hear us there. So we drove from Halifax to Vancouver, playing only Moncton and Winnipeg along the way—that was insane. The night that we played at the Commodore was a showcase night. We went on early, and there might have been only twenty-five or thirty people there, which made for a pretty cavernous experience. We played on borrowed and crappy gear, but the guy from Geffen saw our set, and we signed our first record deal. Things started to happen for us after that, so the Commodore has cemented itself in our band's history. It's definitely my favourite venue in Canada, and I'm glad we've come back over the years regularly to play it.

Nirvana performed at the Commodore twice in 1991. On the first occasion, on March 8, they opened for Seattle band the Screaming Trees. Vancouver broadcaster and writer Grant Lawrence recalls, "The hype [for Nirvana] was building then, and it seemed obvious that Nirvana should headline, but they were embarrassed at the suggestion. It was a sold-out massive, epic show that night." Photo above, October 30, 1991: Kevin Statham

Above and right: Prominent Seattle photographer
Charles Peterson, who often toured with Nirvana,
photographed the band at the Commodore Ballroom in
1991. "I remember that the band was relaxed and had a
good time," he says. "Some of the photos of that night
went on to become signature live shots of Nirvana."
Photos: Charles Peterson

The Screaming Trees and Nirvana, 1991.
Courtesy of Neptoon Records Archives

Jay Ferguson of Sloan at the Commodore, 1996; Noel Gallagher during Oasis's Commodore appearance, January 29, 1995. Photos: Kevin Statham

Sloan keyboardist Gregory Macdonald had a special connection to the ballroom long before he attended shows in the 1990s or had the opportunity to perform there. MacDonald is the grandson of musician George Calangis, the bandleader in the Commodore's house orchestra in the 1940s and '50s. "He died when my mother was a teenager, but he looms large in my family, and I've always felt a connection to him," says Macdonald. "Every time I'm there, I feel like I'm hanging out with him, he knows that I'm there, and I'm getting to know him. The Commodore was such a big part of his life. It's always been an important place for me, and while I've had the chance to play at a lot of great rooms over the years, the Commodore's still my favourite in the world."

While the Commodore was witness to Vancouver's changing music scene, its downstairs neighbours on Granville Street also got to see some of the action. Formerly the Mall Book Bazaar, the Granville Book Company opened under new management in 1986 and was a great place to hang out for those who didn't have tickets but wanted to hear the show, because the store was located immediately beneath the front part of the Commodore's dance floor. On a quiet night in the bookstore, browsers could actually hear stage banter. During a sold-out show, the deafening pounding of a thousand pairs of feet on the dance floor echoed through the rafters of the bookstore, sounding like a ship's hull being repeatedly hit.

Regular bookstore patrons, used to the sound, would continue to calmly browse through the stacks, while newcomers could look nervous when, as former store operator Jim Allen recalls, "the fluorescent lights in the bookstore would swing back and forth, and books would fall off shelves. One night, concrete fell from the ceiling and smashed down in pieces about the size of your fist. People rushed out of the store thinking that the ceiling was finally going to crash through. But the next day was "business as usual for us down there." Next to the Bon Ton Bakery, Terry MacFarlane operated the Tandy Leather Shop beneath the Commodore in the 1980s and early '90s, selling leather craft supplies. Sometimes, musicians booked to play at the Commodore would go to his shop before their shows to get leather guitar straps repaired. "Back then, before there were so many panhandlers down there and rents went up, there was still a good mix of foot traffic on Granville Street," MacFarlane recalls. Most memorable for him were the Dogwood Monarchist Society Coronation balls held annually at the Commodore. At these gay balls, an Emperor and Empress were crowned and the monies raised were given to charities. MacFarlane remembers that, "all day, limos pulled up to the club, and people in costume were coming and going. It was quite a sight to see."

On other nights, limousines pulled up to the Commodore's back door delivering VIPs who came to see the shows. Stagehand Tim Tilton has plenty of stories he can tell and even more that he can't repeat about celebrities at the Commodore. One of his favourites is from 1995, when actor Gary Busey came to the Cheap Trick show.

> Drew called me into his office one night and there sat Gary Busey. He was in town filming a movie, and Drew asked me to take care of him. Busey already knew Robin Zander and Rick Neilsen from Cheap Trick, so I brought him back-stage and he partied with them before the show. I remember

In 1995, actor Gary Busey, in Vancouver to shoot a movie, came to see Cheap Trick at the Commodore and apparently failed to make it to set the following day. Poster: Courtesy of Live Nation Archive

Chuck Prudham began working as a stagehand at the Ballroom in 1991 and has many memories of his time there. A particular favourite is the night that ex-KISS guitarist Ace Frehley and drummer Peter Criss returned to the Commodore in July 1995 under the banner of their Bad Boys of KISS tour:

The show was over, and we were packing stuff out. One of the local crew had a girlfriend who was a stripper, and at the end of the night, while we were loading out, she sat on a stool by the backstage door waiting for her boyfriend to finish up. All of the crew guys were hitting on her, but she wasn't listening to them. Then I see Ace Frehley walk over to her. Without saying a word, he stops in front of her, takes out a felt pen, puts his hands gently on her knees, spreads her legs apart, autographs the inside of her leg, smiles, shuts her legs, and goes out the back door. It was a ridiculously rock 'n' roll thing to do! I don't know who was more speechless, Ace, the girl, or me.

the first drink he ordered was a quadruple rum and coke, and I thought, *Oh man, it's going to start like this*. He was backstage there all night with them and watched the show from the side of the stage. He was still partying with the band after the show while we loaded out.

The next morning, I get up early and turn the radio on, and I hear [station DJ] Brother Jake say, "Oh, by the way, if anybody has seen Gary Busey this morning, give us a call, because word has it he didn't show up on set!" I remembered that Gary and the band were on the tour bus still going at it when I left. So when the bus left, he probably had no idea and carried on partying until the next town. I called the station and told them, "You want to know where Gary Busey is? Try Seattle."

45 Harrison, Tom. "End of Era with Pump's Passing," *The Province*, July 13, 1997.

46 McDonald, Verne. "Strummer Leads a Pogue-o Party," *Georgia Straight*, October 11–19, 1991, 39.

While it's not widely recognized, the Commodore was, for a time, used as a venue for stand-up comedy in Vancouver. Jay Leno and Jerry Seinfeld did headlining shows there in 1986 and 1987, and even Henny Youngman appeared on the Commodore stage in 1988. Sam Kinison performed there on March 26, 1992 in one of his last shows before he was killed in an automobile accident just a few weeks later. Poster courtesy of Neptoon Records Archives. Jerry Seinfeld ad courtesy of the *Georgia Straight*.

The World Famous
COMMODORE
BALLROOM
FOR SALE
Contact: Kerry Rawlick
Realty Executives
Office: 588-9955 • Fax: 588-9562 • Cel: 813-0318

{ Vancouver concert audiences were shocked to
read that the Commodore was for sale in 1996.
Courtesy of the *Georgia Straight* }

TORN UP AND TORN OUT

Fourteen

AFTER DECADES OF wear and tear, the Commodore's stage was beginning to bounce as much as its dance floor. In 1994, during a performance by Courtney Love's band Hole, Drew Burns noticed that the microphone stand was tilting even more unnaturally than Love, and a few months later, singer-songwriter Ani DiFranco struggled to perform with a wobbling microphone stand that nearly hit her in the mouth.

The source of the instability was determined to be a cracked beam underneath the stage, and while Burns first hoped it would be just the beam that needed to be replaced, on further examination it became apparent that the entire floor needed renovation. Burns decided to put in a new floor. After soaking up more than sixty years of music, cocktails, and dancing feet, the legendary Commodore Ballroom floor was removed on January 3, 1996.

When the boards were pulled up, the Ballroom revealed a few treasures that had been sealed in the floor since 1930. A pearl and gold chain that had slipped down beneath the floorboards and a few spent bottles of Canadian rye, cigarette packs, and brown paper nail bags with the name "Gaston" written on them

in pencil were discovered. But the room's most tantalizing secret was what had given the floor its infamous bounce and shock-absorbing, characteristic spring. This was revealed to be a web of shiplap, two-by-threes, and batts of horsehair and car tires.

Replicating the craftsmanship and materials required to build a new version of the floor was prohibitively costly; installing horsehair ballroom floors had become a lost art in the sixty years since the Commodore's had been constructed. And while Gaston himself had long been unavailable to help with this renovation, BC Hardwood Flooring, the same family business that laid the original floor, was on hand to install the new one. It took three days to lay down the floor, made of plywood, two layers of drywall and one of cork, and two-by-threes and two-by-sixes that rested on foam rubber.

The old floor wasn't consigned to the trash heap, however. Drew Burns was aware of the public's interest in and sentimental feelings about the fabled dance floor. In connection with CFOX radio, he organized an event to cut sections of the floor into squares and sell them. Proceeds would benefit the BC Children's Hospital. One square foot was priced at thirty dollars, four square feet at $100, and nine square feet cost $250. Each section came with a small plaque that identified it as the "Commodore Ballroom Dance Floor 1929–1995" and a letter of authenticity. In all, $20,000 was raised as 400 people—including an eighty-year-old man who'd met his wife at the Commodore when he was twenty-one, a rock music fan who planned to use the wood to construct a guitar, and *Georgia Straight* editor Charles Campbell, who purchased a large piece that he installed as his new dining room floor—each took home a piece of Commodore history.

After more than three weeks of being closed, Britpop band Blur reopened the Commodore, headlining a sold-out show, with local group Pluto opening. That night, a full house of 1,000 patrons christened the new flooring and danced to Damon Albarn's "woo-hoo" chorus in Blur's hit "Song 2," while downstairs at the Granville Book Company, only a handful of books fell off the shelves. The new floor didn't have the same bounce as the old one, though some said it would take a few years to get "worked in," as the old floor's spring was the result of decades of use. But this would seem trivial compared to what faced the Commodore next.

Stagehand Chuck Prudham recalls that, not long after the Commodore reopened in 1995, "Drew said to me, 'Hey, Chuck, I'm going on vacation for a couple of weeks. Take care of this and that for me while I'm away.' When he came back, and I asked how the vacation had gone, he discreetly opened his shirt up and showed me the scar tissue down his chest." Burns hadn't gone on vacation, but instead had gone into the hospital for heart surgery. "He didn't tell any of us," Prudham says, "and he just wanted to keep it to himself. The doctors told him that he could either become the first ghost of the Commodore or he could retire. I don't think he wanted to give it up, but that's probably when he first thought about selling the place."

Despite years of sixteen-hour days and investing his own money in the room, it had rewarded Burns. He'd bought a yacht in Vancouver's False Creek, and a condo in Hawaii. But now the business was changing. There weren't as many bands filling the room regularly, and the ones who did wanted higher performance guarantees. Although Burns had seen many cycles in which the business was down and then bounced back, there was no denying that it now cost more to operate the room—and there was no ignoring the fact that he was getting older. The late nights had added up, and he needed to take better care of himself.

While Burns' company Commodore Cabaret Ltd. owned the liquor license, the business, and an estimated $200,000 of fixtures and decorations, the Commodore building itself was owned by an Ontario-based company called Pensionfund Realty Ltd. and administered by the equity firm Morguard, which had purchased the building directly from the Reifel family in 1974. Burns hoped to sell the business as well as the liquor license simultaneously to a new buyer at the figure he reasoned it was worth. While the business and fixtures were certainly valuable, it was the Commodore's "grandfathered" liquor license, a combined liquor and food license that the provincial liquor control board no longer issued, that was of particular value.

When Burns' lease, last renewed in 1986, ended on December 31, 1995, he agreed to a four-month extension while he continued to seek a buyer.[47] But a protracted legal battle ensued, with Burns claiming that Morguard tried to go around him to get a new owner with their own liquor license. Morguard claimed that they had lost patience with Burns who, they stated in court, failed to present them with potential offers. But in what seemed the most damning accusation, Morguard claimed that Burns had overvalued the Commodore's assets. It felt as if the company, thousands of miles away in Ontario, looked at their balance sheets and lowered the value of his life's work.

In June 1996, an injunction filed by Burns' lawyer Bruce Redekop went to the Supreme Court of British Columbia in a case presided over by Justice Wally Oppal. Burns believed that Morguard had made a verbal agreement to give him a month-to-month lease and hoped that an injunction would give him more time to sell under his own terms. But Justice Oppal, finding no evidence of a lease extensions or agreements in place, reluctantly ruled against him, stating in his conclusion, "I am most sympathetic to the concerns and the plight of the Commodore. Much has been said about the Commodore's storied past and its place in the social and cultural history of this city. However, it is not the function of a court of law to substitute an agreement between the parties where no agreement has been made."[48]

During the hearing, a number of potential offers that had been fielded by Morguard came to light, including an offer by the Ross Patterson Group, a Texas-based company that operated a string of clubs in the US called "Live in America." There were fears that they could turn the Commodore into a stars-and-stripes-themed rock 'n' roll pool room with a burger menu. An offer from Calgary nightclub owner Paul Vickers, who ran a successful country music bar called Cowboys, ignited concern that the room would be gutted and a mechanical bull installed. Vancouver city councillor Lynne Kennedy tried to assuage the public's fears that the Commodore would undergo a wholesale change. "We want to ensure that the Commodore continues in the way that it always has, as a live music venue."[49]

But Burns' days were done. He admitted in interviews given at the time that he would miss the Ballroom, and said that it felt like he'd been married to it for twenty-seven years.

A host of jazz legends appeared at the Commodore as part of the annual Vancouver International Jazz Festival, including Sonny Rollins in 1993. Photo: Kevin Statham

"You have to put love into a building," he told the *Georgia Straight*. "Because love is something that people can feel. Your staff and everybody who works in the place have to understand that instinctively. Otherwise, you could pour millions of dollars into it and all you'd get back would be bricks and mortar."[50]

With the closure, a deluge of well-wishers came forward. No living nightclub operator in the city's history before or since has garnered the same outpouring of heartfelt appreciation. Many people said that Burns' own unique character was what defined the Commodore. Hundreds of musicians, agents, promoters, reporters, and Commodore regulars thanked him for everything he'd done for the music scene in Vancouver, and some viewed his departure as "the day the music died." Most saddened, perhaps, was the club's close-knit staff, many of whom had worked with Burns for decades. Stagehand Chuck Prudham said that "it felt like Drew got shoved out. It wasn't the way he should have been treated. That man did more for me than my own father."

While the court heard the remaining claims, the Vancouver International Jazz Festival brought a week of performances to the Commodore, featuring bands like NRBQ, BeauSoleil, and Maceo Parker. But on July 12, 1996, the Commodore Ballroom closed its doors, and Drew Burns returned the keys he'd first picked up in 1969.

The closure of the Commodore Ballroom was unquestionably detrimental to the local concert landscape, especially because there were no comparable venues of its size in Vancouver to replace it. "When the Commodore closed, up-and-coming acts didn't have a really great place to play in Vancouver," says musician Jim Byrnes. "The place was an anchor for [bands doing] western Canadian tours; if they couldn't anchor four or five nights in a proper place, they just quit coming—and, it seemed, they forgot we were here."

While there were still local civic theatres in which to perform, manager Bruce Allen explains that, "it's a great vibe at the Commodore when its packed—there's nothing quite like it, with the audience standing right in front of a stage that's low to the ground. It's much better than any theatre that way. A lot of acts would rather have played the Commodore than the theatres."

The closure of the Commodore signalled a particularly dark period for local bands too. Less than a year later, the Town Pump closed as well, only to reopen as a DJ dance club called Sonar. Local bands were left to play either 200-person capacity pubs like the Railway Club, Marine Club, or Piccadilly Pub, which were too small, or the 2,700-person Orpheum Theatre, which was too big. Other clubs (the Starfish Room, the Gate, the Brickyard) tried to fill the gap, but none lasted. Richards on Richards, better known as a nightclub, even made an unexpected emergence as a popular live music room. But none of these venues had what the Commodore had—good sightlines, a great dance floor, a special atmosphere, and the history—and without a room for great bands to play in, the buzz bands lost their buzz and disbanded or moved away. The same fate that had befallen the Cave, the Palomar Ballroom, Marco Polo, Oil Can Harry's, and many other fabled Vancouver nightclubs seemed to have taken the Commodore too.

For the next three years, Vancouverites who walked down Granville Street passed the Commodore's once welcoming front double doors, now locked and tagged by graffiti artists. As the late writer Dave Watson observed, "The entrance—two small doors, a step and a sign—will be shut. It's incredible how those two small doors can leave such a huge gap in the city of Vancouver when they're locked up tight. Until they're open again, we can only remember."[51]

47 Smith, Charlie. "Battle For Ballroom Drags On," *Georgia Straight,* July 4–11, 1996, 8.

48 Commodore Cabaret Ltd. vs. Pensionfund Properties Ltd., June 27, 1996, 3024. (British Columbia Supreme Court, Vancouver Registry, C962642, Item 29.)

49 Monk, Katherine. "Commodore Decision Today," *Vancouver Sun*, June 27, 1996, A2.

50 Lekich, John. "The Ballroom's Modest Prince," *Georgia Straight*, July 11–18, 1996 15–16.

51 Watson, Dave. "Denizens Remember the Great Times and Bums Rushes," *Georgia Straight*, July 11–18, 1996.

The Commodore Ballroom, 2014.
Photo: Jamie Taylor/concertaddicts.com

THE NEW SHOWMEN

Fifteen

IN 1999, VANCOUVER manager Bruce Allen and his business partner Roger Gibson acquired the ballroom's liquor license and, partnered with Universal Concerts, made a successful bid to purchase the Commodore. Halfway through the process, Seagram-owned Universal Concerts was sold to House of Blues Concerts. While there were concerns that the Ballroom was essentially being taken over by a large American corporation, only an entity with the financial clout of a large corporation had the resources to run the Commodore. The local House of Blues Concerts office, especially Kevin Donnelly, managed the venue, but it was then partially owned by Molson Breweries, and the provincial liquor act stipulated that Molson, as a distributor, couldn't also hold a liquor license. So Allen and Gibson owned the license, and House of Blues was primed to run the business.

When the Commodore had closed in 1996 after more than sixty-five years of dances, parties, and concerts, it was generally acknowledged that the room was showing its age. "If you happened to be there in the daytime and got a good look around, it didn't look great," says John Armstrong. "You

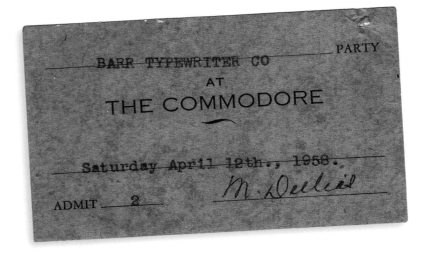

Commodore party ticket, 1958, discovered forty years later. Courtesy of Tim Tilton

realized how ratty and worn out it was beginning to look." House of Blues put $4 million into the renovations. The dance floor that Burns installed in 1996 remained, but the rest of the Commodore's interior was gutted to redesign the room. The renovation revealed more treasures left behind by carpenters from previous eras hidden behind the walls and in the rafters. Along with some old stubby beer bottles and cigarette packs, a soldier's helmet from World War I and a ticket to the Barr Typewriter Company Party on April 12, 1958, signed by Marion Dillias, were also discovered, as well as a large wall-length mirror that had been covered over.

While the rebuilding of the room was underway, there were equally important decisions to be made about who was going to run it. The days of a single owner-operator like Burns running a nightclub of this size were over; the expenses and demands of the job were more than one person could handle. The kind of people involved in running nightclubs had changed as well. Where once colourful, cigar-chomping characters with look-them-in-the-eye handshakes were typical nightclub proprietors, many of the new bar managers were fresh-faced youths with hospitality degrees from vocational colleges and food and beverage internships from resort hotels.

But not all. Before Gord Knights found himself standing behind the bar at the Town Pump, he was behind a microscope in a lab. Knights had a degree in genetics and came to Vancouver to work in a lab, but found the job less appealing than running a bar. "There's not much you can take from genetics to running a bar, but it is more fun," he reveals. When the Town Pump closed in 1997, Knights was considering a career change when a call came from Roger Gibson and the

House of Blues partnership to see if he would be interested in running the Commodore. Knights says that the legacy of Drew Burns cast a long shadow. "I always viewed Drew as royalty, a real king."

Drew Burns' office, 1995. Photo: Keven Statham

> After work at the Town Pump, I used to visit Drew in his office with Mel Warner or Bob Burrows, and you'd see the history of the room on his walls, all the posters and signed pictures, the safe open with a stack of cash, a tumbler of whiskey on his desk—he was a one-man show. He had a lot of people around him, but it was apparent that he was the one driving the ship.
>
> I saw him when he was successful in the business, but also some of the decline. It was apparent to me that even if you were a thirty-year veteran of the business, and you were somebody like Drew—who made things happen like nobody else could—and he could go down swinging, then certainly we could fail completely. If we somehow tripped ourselves up, we might just permanently shut the doors on the Commodore.

Despite his misgivings, Knights took the job and immediately jumped in to deal with permits, health inspections, licensing, and bar-operations issues. "We had to hire and train 100 staff in about eight days; we had a cattle call of 3,000 interviews. We had shows booked and sold out before hiring a single bartender, so we needed to get the right people, right away," Knights says.

The Commodore also still needed someone to take on the duty of booking the bands. Like so many before him, Jason

The Cramps featuring Poison Ivy on guitar, with a rare shot of vocalist Lux Interior in the background at the Commodore on April 12, 1999. Photo: Kevin Statham

Grant's first experience at the Commodore was of sneaking in when he was underaged to see a show. It was April 1984 and Grant, then just sixteen and working as a DJ at CiTR radio, managed to get on the guest list for a concert by one of his favourite bands, the Cramps. He hoped that being on the list would mean he wasn't ID'ed by the doormen, but decided not to leave it to chance. "As a date, I brought one of the prettiest, more mature-looking DJs from the station, and I even wore a shirt and tie so I'd look old enough. I remember the 'You gotta be kidding me' look on face of the guy at the door; I looked twelve when I was sixteen, but I got in!" he laughs. The Cramps were at or near their peak then, and Grant recalls that "it was an absolutely transformative event for me to see that band in their prime. It felt like being connected on the hotline back to the origins of rock 'n' roll. Afterward, I had a real desire to always be around music."

Grant eventually found work in the marketing department of MCA Concerts before the merger with House of Blues Concerts. But when the company got involved in the reopening of the Commodore, Grant had reservations. "The Commodore had been created by people with no corporate background, and I thought there was some danger that it would be remodelled by a company instead of an individual." But when initial candidates for the club's new talent-buyer position were unavailable or not interested, thirty-one-year-old Grant was unexpectedly promoted as the new Commodore talent buyer. "It was unimaginable to me that they'd hand something that important to someone who had never done the job before. I was intimidated, but I knew I was going to throw everything I had at it, and if it failed, it wouldn't be from lack of trying."

Born and raised in Vancouver, Grant knew what Drew Burns had brought to the building. "I went for lunch with Drew before I took the job," he says, "almost to ask for his blessing. We had a good long talk, and he was kind and supportive. I knew how much the place was his baby, so I felt awkward being the stepfather. But he gave me the names of a few people I should talk to right away from the Jazz Festival, and I got ten days of the next year booked, so I just had to worry about the other 355!"

When the Commodore reopened on November 12, 1999, Blue Rodeo christened the new stage along with local opening act Sharkskin. The event was the lead on the local TV evening news; this was not a just a story about the reopening of a business, it undeniably emphasized that the Commodore had been vital and integral for the people of Vancouver, that something important had been missing while it was closed, but it was back again.

In the opening weeks, however, some Ballroom regulars bristled at the renovations. The dated-looking lights and décor, like the illuminated columns filled with bubbles and "spaceship" balcony, were removed in the renovation, and some felt that the club had lost its old charm. Perhaps it was just surprising to see the Commodore looking polished and new. The renovations had brought back the classic design of the ballroom so that it more closely resembled how it looked at its opening in 1930 with signature Art Deco metal trim and cherrywood panelling. "I know it needed fixing up," says Jim Byrnes. "But the ghosts that hung around were part of the fun, and to me, a few too many of the cobwebs were swept away."

Blue Rodeo singer and guitarist Jim Cuddy had a slightly different opinion. "You hate to see the vestiges of the old room

Blue Rodeo has performed nearly thirty times at the Commodore since 1989. In January 1993, the "Blue Rodeo and Friends" concert featured local guests including Barney Bentall and Neil Osborne of 54-40 playing with the band. "I remember playing with Sarah McLachlan that night," recalls Jim Cuddy, "and the songs we did with her really stick out in my mind." Greg Keelor recalls a "really shambolic rock' n' roll take on the Replacements' 'Bastards of Young' led by Vancouver punk icon Art Bergmann." Photos: Kevin Stratham

Above: Rob Wright (bass)
and John Wright (drums) of
Nomeansno onstage in 1995.
Photo: Kevin Statham

Right: Jim Cuddy has played
with Blue Rodeo and solo at
the Commodore many times;
he's shown here onstage in
2006. Poster courtesy of Live
Nation Poster Archive

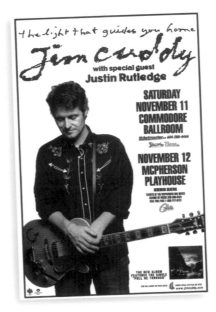

go. There was sort of a beautiful grottiness to it, but it couldn't have lasted like that. The old room had its disadvantages. The sound onstage was very dense, but you overlooked it because the room had a great crowd reaction. With the gear they have and the techs working there now, it's totally pro. It feels like it could last another sixty-five years."

"There had been a lot of innovations in PA systems before we reopened," says Commodore technical director Byron Lonneberg, who joined the Commodore at the same time Gord Knights signed on. Lonneberg was responsible for implementing the club's new audio and visual equipment. "I pushed hard for what was then a new, innovative, line-array PA system that allows you to focus the sound rather than have it bounce around the ceiling. It makes the room sound better, and it's a quarter the size of the old gear," he says. "It's held up well. Having and maintaining top technical equipment is a big part of what we tried to do to enhance the legacy."

In the weeks after it reopened, the Commodore welcomed back both a host of favourite bands who considered it a second home and Canadian bands new to the venue, and before the year was over, 54-40, Big Sugar, Colin James, Wide Mouth Mason, Nomeansno, Doug and the Slugs, Platinum Blonde, and Spirit of the West performed there. It was at a Spirit of the West show that the ground-floor stores were once again all too aware of their upstairs neighbour. During the closure, some of the retail stores had closed over the small vents above their front doorways. These vents had been designed to release the air pressure generated by the dance floor upstairs. So when 1,000 pairs of Doc Martens pogoed on the Commodore's floor, the windows and doors of the stores below it nearly blew open because the air pressure wasn't able to "exhale" through the now-covered vents. Who knew that the Ballroom had its own lungs?

The Commodore was back. In Jason Grant's first couple of years, bands including NOFX, Fishbone, Jeff Healey, Richard Thompson, Warren Zevon, the Cowboy Junkies, the Matthew Good Band, Richard Ashcroft, Ween, Maceo Parker, and Midnight Oil all performed on the Commodore stage, as well as local stalwarts like D.O.A. And when the Cramps returned to the Commodore in 2000, Jason Grant was the one booking them. "After the show, Lux was soft-spoken and very kind," Grant says. "I wanted to tell them they were my inspiration for being around music. It was a wonderful thing to get to tell him that before he passed away."

Grant recalls other shows that stood out for him in those years. "The White Stripes show in 2002 was explosive from start to finish. The opening act was a band called Whirlwind Heat—unconventional noise rock that put people on edge. Anyone who came down that night to see the flavour of the week was pretty unsettled," he recalls. "And then the White Stripes came on and destroyed the place. They were one of a few bands that were on a continuum with bands like the Cramps and a handful of others; they were part of the roots and soul of rock 'n' roll. It was inspiring, and it felt like a corner was being turned. The Strokes show the year earlier had the same effect, but more emotionally detached onstage—saying the same thing with not as many exclamation marks."

For Gord Knights, one of the most memorable events in the early years after the reopening was when Coldplay came to Vancouver for their North American debut at the Commodore Ballroom.

"The White Stripes show in 2002 was explosive from start to finish," recalls then Commodore talent buyer Jason Grant. Photos: Kevin Statham

Clockwise from top left: The Cowboy Junkies in 2000, Courtesy of Live Nation Poster Archive; The Matthew Good Band performed two back-to-back sold-out nights at the Commodore followed by two sold-out nights at the Vogue Theatre in 2003, Courtesy of Live Nation Poster Archive; Richard Thompson. Courtesy of Live Nation Poster Archive; Courtesy of Live Nation Poster Archive; Midnight Oil's Peter Garrett, November 16, 2001, Photo: Kevin Statham

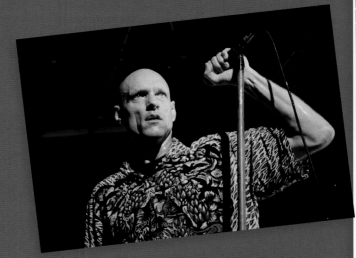

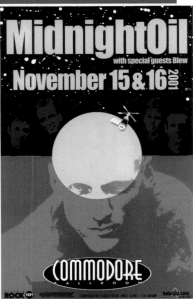

I didn't know that much about them. They were a new band. I was at the Commodore during the day, and there wasn't much going on in the afternoon. Sometimes I like to sit out in the room with my laptop rather than at my desk, and [Coldplay singer] Chris Martin came in. The piano had arrived a couple of hours before the rest of their gear. He saw me in the corner and said, "Hey, you don't mind if I play the piano for a while, do you?" I said, "As long as you don't mind if I listen!" The piano wasn't miked, but he just wanted to get comfortable with it, the stage, and the space. But as I worked away, he played their whole first album start to finish. Just the two of us were there. I remember thinking, *This is amazing, this is going to be so big.* At the end, he got up and yelled over, "Well, how was that?" I said something to the effect of, "You guys are going to be huge," and he just laughed. The show was great that night. Weeks later, when they went back to the UK, they played to 90,000 people at Wembley. So it was amazing to catch them then and be an audience of one that afternoon.

In subsequent years, Grant kept the Commodore concert calendar filled with a litany of bands, including Pearl Jam, Thievery Corporation, the New Pornographers, Neko Case, Lucinda Williams, Steve Earle, Guided by Voices, the Flaming Lips, the Violent Femmes, Bad Religion, Billy Bragg, Motörhead, Nickelback, Morcheeba, and local classic-rock favourites like Loverboy, Trooper, and Prism. But one of his favourite events was the Discotronic "Disco Nights," organized and hosted by DJ Chiclet and MC Velvet K, who spun retro disco records to capacity crowds dressed

Above: Lemmy of Mötorhead, May 13, 2002. Photo: Kevin Statham

Left: The immensely popular Discotronic retro disco nights at the Commodore between 2000 and 2004 proved the longest-running club nights in Vancouver. Courtesy of Live Nation Poster Archive

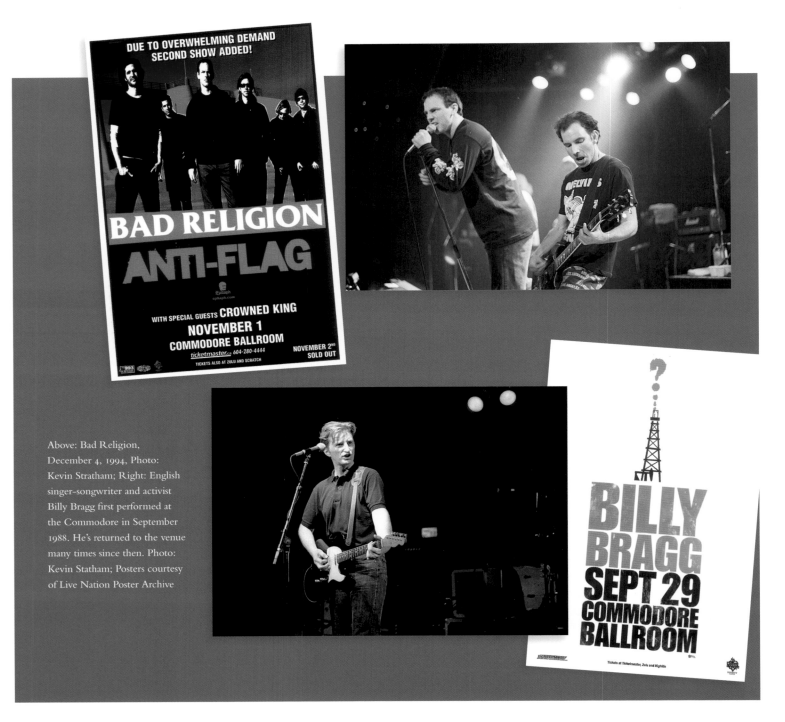

Above: Bad Religion, December 4, 1994, Photo: Kevin Stratham; Right: English singer-songwriter and activist Billy Bragg first performed at the Commodore in September 1988. He's returned to the venue many times since then. Photo: Kevin Statham; Posters courtesy of Live Nation Poster Archive

in disco-era style clothing every Tuesday night in the early 2000s. "That was a costume party every week," recalls Grant. "I don't know if disco was that popular the first time around in Vancouver! There was some combination of the venue and the music happening, and [there wasn't] another club night in the city's history that was that big for that long."

The Commodore celebrated its seventy-fifth anniversary in 2004. Afterward, it was discovered that this was actually the Commodore's seventy-fourth birthday. The mistake seemed to originate with long-deceased bookkeeper Marion Dillias, who maintained that the Commodore had closed not long after it opened because of the Great Depression. "Marion said for sure it was December 3," said Drew Burns. "And Doug Gourlay told me the same thing." While the decision to build the Commodore began in 1929, as building records and newspapers show, it opened on December 3, 1930. The disparity in the date didn't dampen the anniversary celebrations, which were marked with a year-long series of performances featuring Ben Harper, Moby, and big band leader Dal Richards, who played the ballroom's birthday on December 3.

The biggest concert at the Commodore during that year, however, was Tom Waits' on October 16. Waits performed the night before at the Orpheum Theatre, and the next evening's performance marked his first club show in two decades. To prevent ticket scalpers from seizing and reselling tickets, they were made available only for pickup and entry by those who had bought them. Many Waits fans camped out on the street the night before to ensure they got the best spots. Those who did were rewarded by being so close to Waits onstage that they could tell the time on his wristwatch. As reviewer Mike Usinger from the *Georgia Straight* noted:

> What made the night a stunner was the way that performer and audience fed off each other's energy. The connection, which never quite happened at the Orpheum, was made early on, right around the middle of "Don't Go into the Barn"… Waits bellowed and spat his way through the story of Everett Lee, who's high on potato-and-tulip wine, and Saginaw Calinda, who lives in the shadow of a long-dead farm. It was at the end of the tune that performer and audience become one. Sounding like a crazy uncle who's been locked in the root cellar for too long, Waits hollered out the line, "Did you cover your tracks?" at which point the crowd screamed back, "Yes, sir."
>
> "Did you bring your knife?"
> "Yes, sir."
> "Did they see your face?"
> "No, sir."
> "Did the mom see you?"
> "No, sir."

And so it went. "Don't Go into the Barn" gave every fan in attendance a memory they'll never forget. Just as amazing was that the show never slowed down after that five-minute masterpiece. Yes, it was that magical.

In 2004, after he'd been nominated for a Pollstar Award the year before as Nightclub Talent Buyer of the Year, Jason Grant moved to Toronto to take a senior position at House of Blues Concerts. "I booked [the Commodore] for five years,

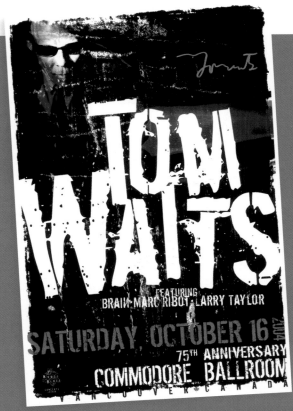

Clockwise from top left: The legendary 2004 Tom Waits concert at the Commodore was his first club date in two decades. Courtesy of Live Nation Poster Archive; Tom Waits at The Commodore. Photo courtesy of Rebecca Blissett; Tom Waits backstage pass, 2004, Courtesy of Tim Tilton

and I'd done what I set out to do," Grant says. "We got the Commodore back on the radar for touring bands. It was time to move on. And I thought we got the best guy in the country to take over."

Erik Hoffman was an emerging concert promoter at Barrymore's Music Hall in Ottawa. He was also a tour manager and soundman for a variety of Canadian bands like Sarah Harmer, Sam Roberts, the Mahones, and Punchbuggy, a job that exposed him to a variety of venues across North America. Although he was thousands of miles away from Vancouver, Hoffman was "very aware of the Commodore Ballroom. I tried to model some of the stuff I did at Barrymore's on what going on [at the Commodore] then. I knew more about the Commodore than I knew about some rooms in Toronto," he says.

In 2004, while on tour in Toronto, Hoffman got talking with House of Blues' Riley O'Connor between a sound check and show time. At some point during their conversation, he realized that the informal chat was essentially a job interview for the position of talent buyer at the Commodore Ballroom. "I was at a fork in the road between being on tour and being a concert promoter in Ottawa," Hoffman recalls. "I needed to pick one or the other, and I thought to myself, *I don't want to book another club in this country unless it's the Commodore*. It's the crown jewel of Canada; it means a lot to so many bands, and I wanted to be a part of it."

It was the kind of leap of faith that O'Connor and Norman Perry had made more than twenty-five years earlier, and found equally as challenging. From the other end of the country, Hoffman had no deep connections to bands in the Vancouver

Muse at the Commodore, 2004, Courtesy of Live Nation Poster Archive; Paul Westerberg's band the Replacements performed at the Commodore in 1989, but he returned to play solo in 1993 and 2005. Courtesy of Live Nation Poster Archive

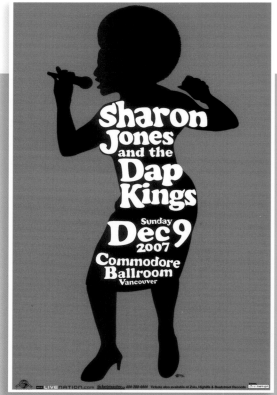

Clockwise from top left: The Roots performed two shows
in one night at the Commodore on November 9, 2005.
They later became the house band on NBC TV show *Late
Night with Jimmy Fallon* and followed Fallon when he became
host of *The Tonight Show*. Courtesy of Live Nation Poster
Archive; "I've seen everybody from Sharon Jones to Gwar
to the Three Six Mafia at the Commodore," says Vancouver
restaurateur and social activist Mark Brand. "I became friends
with the Sharon Jones band after their [2007] show. The
Commodore has a real feel of community and history to it.
I think it's one of the best venues in the Pacific Northwest."
Courtesy of Live Nation Poster Archive; Snoop Dogg,
December 2002, Photo: Kevin Statham

music scene. "It was intimidating," he says. "I came out with a lot of piss and vinegar because that's how I am, but it was hard that first year. There's a really big disconnect between eastern and western local music scenes ... I was coming from being an emerging player in Ontario to running the most important room in Vancouver. I leaned a lot from Jason in that first year. I had so much respect for what the room meant to people, and what I had to accomplish wasn't lost on me."

Hoffman also notes that not being as emotionally attached to the Commodore could be an advantage; when events that had become annual traditions at the ballroom reluctantly needed to be discontinued, it was easier for him to do so. "Everything runs its course, and when it does, you have to know when to pull the plug," he says.

New elements were also becoming a part of the concert business, like the increased significance of social media. If patrons of the Commodore in the 1930s couldn't have imagined slam dancing and moshing, one wonders what they would have thought seeing the room full of people holding up mobile phones and taking pictures. "Watching the show though a camera phone is a little ridiculous to me," says Hoffman. "Are you really going to go back and look at these, or try to enjoy the show while you're right in front of it? I kind of enjoy it when I hear some bands onstage tease audiences about that! But the nice thing about social media is that you can announce a surprise show three hours beforehand, or if the band gets stuck at the border and can't get through, we can inform people right away."

Hoffman booked the Commodore from 2004 to 2012, and recalls some favourite shows from those years. "The Roots

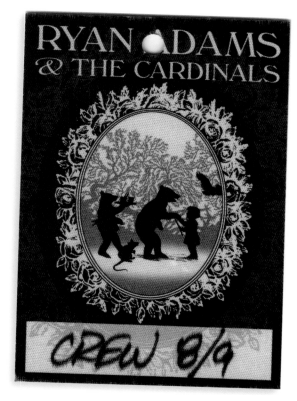

Vancouver's Juno award-winning singer-songwriter Dan Mangan was at the 2007 Ryan Adams show. "I remember being pretty drunk that night, and even though I was a huge Ryan Adams fan, I yelled out, "Play 'Cuts like a Knife!' It's a huge no-no to play the Bryan/Ryan Adams card, and everyone stared at me like I was a total asshole (which I admittedly was). Ryan just looked me square in the eye and said over the mic, "Hey, man, I can get a new lawyer, but you can't get a new face when I punch yours!" Then he proceeded to get totally fucked up, fire his band onstage, climb up the speaker stack, and narrowly avoid falling face-first into the audience. What a legend. Love that guy." Ryan Adams backstage pass, 2007, courtesy of Tim Tilton

Erik Hoffman, 2014. Photo: courtesy of Live Nation Concerts

shows were great. Jurassic 5 was over the top. A lot of the hip hop shows, acts that had a conscientious undertone like Michael Franti, were also great, and we did multiple nights. Snoop Dogg has come to play the Ballroom for just about every record he's done, even when he was an arena act." For Hoffman, "the best thing" is a show like Sharon Jones' first at the Commodore in 2005, when "she just got up and destroyed the place with an amazing set. There's nothing like it! Maybe it's a warm night, there's a little sweat from everybody dancing, and you've had a drink, but something happens in there that doesn't seem to happen in other places so easily. I've seen it happen with opening acts who just nail it too," he says.

But Erik Hoffman sometimes saw things go wrong. As a big fan of Americana artists, he was excited to book Ryan Adams into the Commodore in 2007. "You could tell the tour hadn't been going well," he recalls, "and onstage, Adams said between songs that if the guys in his band had practiced, they might get better." Hoffman was nevertheless looking forward to meeting Adams after the show. "I had a bottle of Dom Pérignon with me, and after the show I thanked him [and gave him the champagne] in the green room. He starts drinking from the bottle on his own while he's talking with me, goes upstairs, fires the band, and the tour is over!"

When people overly venerate the "good old days of music" and insist that music isn't what it used to be, it makes Hoffman bristle. "Nothing screams 'old jaded music guy' more than that," he says.

But I get it that things get embellished over the years, and how concerts tie into people's lives—especially in their youth. We all have ideas about what the best rock 'n' roll period was, but the truth of the matter is that it's still happening, and all we can do is just set the table. The room is still breaking new artists, and there's new history constantly brewing there. I believe it was great in the past, of course it was, but I don't think it's any less classic today. The heart and soul of the Commodore is still alive and well. I can guarantee you that there's somebody in their twenties who is going to see a show there this week and have the best night of their life, one they'll still be talking about when they're forty. Our job is to ensure that keeps going.

Left: Jarvis Cocker at the Commodore in 2007. Vancouver group Choir Practice opened. Courtesy of Live Nation Poster Archive

Right: The Polyphonic Spree, July 13, 2007. Courtesy of Live Nation Poster Archive

{ Outside the Commodore Ballroom,
September 2014. Photo: Jamie Taylor }

Sixteen

It's Saturday night on Granville Street. On weekend nights, when a Vancouver Canucks, BC Lions, or Vancouver Whitecaps game ends, several thousand sports fans will often head from one of the two downtown arenas to the Granville entertainment strip, joining the nightclubbing crowds already there. The police have cordoned off the 900 block of Granville, as they do most Friday and Saturday nights, with an estimated cost to the police department of nearly $1 million a year. While many club-goers move from bar to bar, others stroll the street, taking in the nightlife circus of people lined up outside the clubs or walking on the pavement, singing, yelling, and laughing. On the sidewalk in front of the Roxy nightclub, a group of women in their mid-twenties stare into their mobile phones as they walk, not noticing a group of guys, about the same age or younger, shoving each other and bumping into some other pedestrians. At first it seems a fight will break out, but the rowdy group is just roughhousing among themselves.

If this section of Granville has a reputation as an area frequented only by young, inebriated club-goers who are known for the troubles they bring, it's thanks to a number of

Granville Street, 2013. Photo: Milos Tosic

well-publicized fights in recent years. In late 2013, for example, Boston Bruins hockey player Milan Lucic went for a post-game drink with friends on the Granville strip and was involved in an altercation with an inebriated nightclub patron, and in February 2014, an aggressive young man began kicking some Granville Street panhandlers. Both incidents were captured on cellphone cameras and broadcast on the local nightly news. Even Blackie, the legendary Commodore bouncer who once struck fear into anyone who got on his wrong side, admits that he avoids the street on weekends. "It's changed so much on Granville. There might have been a lot of fights back in the old days, but now you see too many guys who get too drunk and think they're tough." Despite the presence of restaurants and performance venues like the Commodore, the Vogue, and the Orpheum that offer more than just drinking, for many people, the negative incidents have come to broadly define the whole street, and its assumed that each weekend Granville sees the kind of angry, drunk, boisterous crowds who were captured on camera during the notorious June 2011 Stanley Cup riots.

The problems began not long after the Vancouver city council decision in 1997 to create the Granville entertainment district. The city's urban density drive (i.e., condo tower development) pressured bars and nightclubs from neighbouring streets to move onto Granville. The city hoped to revitalize the strip, which had languished since the early-1970s creation of the Granville Mall for pedestrians. Since then, the city has invested $21 million to update the street by removing the old bollards and chains, widening the sidewalks, adding new trees and metallic street benches, and most significantly, installing modern street lighting.

Despite the redesign, it's been suggested that the problems of the entertainment strip go deeper than sidewalk aesthetics; Granville still needs to reassess a business model that caters primarily to nineteen- to twenty-five-year-olds. Most of the news-making incidents have occurred south of the Commodore, and no one is suggesting that audiences avoid attending shows at the Commodore or other concert venues, but it is a long-term concern. Nevertheless, there are those who regard Granville Street after dark with amusement.

"There are cool people at the Commodore who are hardcore music fans, and that's the reason they've made the trek downtown," says *Georgia Straight* music editor Mike Usinger, who regularly reviews concerts there. "But at the end of the night, when you walk down those stairs, you land right on Granville street with all these young, drunk women stumbling in their heels, and testosterone-fuelled guys. I don't think that makes the Commodore any less of a destination. If anything, you can look at it as an oasis of cool," he jokes. "It makes for a fascinating sociological experiment, and the people-watching is the best free show to be found on a Friday night."

A bigger problem than drunken misbehaviour for the future of the Commodore and other downtown concert venues may be the costs of running and maintaining a nightclub in a city where property values and development potential ranks higher than the cultural and heritage significance of some of its buildings. The creation of the Granville entertainment district, after all, coincided with the boom in condominium development and helped to wipe out venues and clubs like the Starfish Room and Richards on Richards, which didn't fit into the new map. But Vancouverites have had to watch this occur all

The Black Keys, April 6, 2008; Gogol Bordello performed three consecutive nights at the Commodore in 2010. Courtesy of Live Nation Poster Archive

Above: Social Distortion singer-guitarist Mike Ness donned a Remembrance Day poppy at this November 9, 2004 performance at the Commodore. Photo: Kevin Stratham

Below: Katy Perry at the Commodore, January 25, 2009. Photo: Michele "Sprout" Neilson.

over the city. In 2013, for example, the Ridge Theatre cinema, which had been in operation for sixty-two years, was torn down and a condominium development built in its place, leaving city heritage advocates to suggest that the city is demolishing its past and leaving its population without theatres, clubs, and entertainment venues for the future. Beyond the loss of old clubs like the Cave or Oil Can Harry's in the 1980s, in more recent years, the Pantages Theatre was demolished after years of neglect, public inaction, and a lack of financing. In 2013, after the Waldorf Hotel's promoters had renovated the bar and restaurant and made it a venue for live music, readings, and art installations, it closed when the owner sold it to a property developer and lease issues arose. The Hollywood Theatre now faces an uncertain future, and the Centre for Performing Arts no longer holds public performances after the evangelical Westside Church purchased the building. Few new venues have opened in the wake of all that's disappeared.

In 2011, *Billboard* magazine named the Commodore one of the ten most influential venues in North America, along with famous clubs like the Fillmore in San Francisco, the 9:30 Club in Washington, DC, and the Troubadour in West Hollywood. *Billboard* did not note that, of all the clubs that made the list, the Commodore Ballroom was the longest-running club used exclusively as a music venue. But the Commodore's importance goes beyond the building's age.

"In the last twenty years, a lot of places like the Commodore have vanished," says musician, producer, and former Atlantic Records A&R executive Tim Sommer. "It used to be common to see a new band play an old theatre; that is, the Kinks or the Stones may have played a club in 1964, and Frank Sinatra sang on the same stage in 1944, and Sarah Bernhardt performed there in the 1920s. There's not a lot of places like that left, especially in North America," he notes. "Places change, the fixtures change, nothing is permanent. But there's something about standing in a room and knowing that, say, both Jimi Hendrix and Charlie Chaplin played there. That's vanished. How many places are even called 'ballrooms' anymore? That's what makes the Commodore such a rarity."

Sommer underscores that it's not just the pedigree of the Commodore building that's unique, but how it relates to its audience and performers alike. "There's a certain magic to know that you've gone through the same front door, up the same staircase, and through the same stage door as legends—particularly as a musician. You have a link with the immediate show business past, but also with a whole century of people who went from city to city doing exactly what you do as a touring musician," says Sommer. "And for an audience, the history and architecture of that room makes the way the bass reverberates off the walls into something remarkable. The Commodore is one of the definitively great rock 'n' roll rooms in the world. And there's only a handful of them left."

"I fear that we are apathetic as a city," says Vancouver musician Simon Kendall. "As a community, we don't care sufficiently to keep these places alive simply for the historical continuity. We've been careless with our history. I remember playing the Cave and thinking, *Duke Ellington played here, Ray Charles played here.* That was in the walls. So many clubs and nightspots are gone now. The fact that the Commodore or even the Penthouse is still there is great. There are so few places like that left."

Because the Commodore Ballroom has been part of Vancouver for so long, it's difficult to imagine the city being forever without it, but we got a taste of that when it closed in 1996 and came close to becoming an American restaurant franchise or country music tavern. Can the same fate that has wiped out so many other venues in Vancouver ever befall the Commodore?

"It's been at risk several times," admits Erik Hoffman of Live Nation. "But if there weren't local people fighting for what it means to the community, the Commodore would be fucking long gone. If somebody came to run it that didn't have an emotional attachment to the place, it could be in danger. Thank God the people who've run it since it opened have all cared deeply about it."

Hoffman notes that the costs of running the Commodore "are astronomical. It's on prime real estate. And to keep up with the latest production needs and have a veteran production staff—we can't scrimp on all of that. It doesn't make good business sense on its own to run the Ballroom," Hoffman says candidly. "But here's the thing. The Commodore is so important for what we do. It's the size of room that allows relationships between bands and promoters to be formed, and those relationships are defining." For bands who no longer draw large audiences, the Ballroom is still a respectable room to play, and audiences get the opportunity to see a performer in a more intimate setting than a large theatre or casino stage. But, as Hoffman explains, the Commodore is an even more important spot for bands before they go on to bigger venues. "When bands sell out the Commodore, it's often at a point when they begin to realize they might be playing arenas next. If, as their

Audio tech Mike Newburg and unidentified stagehand.
Photos: Adam PW Smith

promoter, we're with them both at the Commodore and the arena, that creates an important connection. The successful shows we do at the arenas allow us to take chances on bands in smaller venues, to book new talent, so one feeds the other. The Commodore is at the cornerstone of this process."

In 2013, Hoffman became the senior vice president for talent for Live Nation Canada and is primarily tasked with putting on multiple outdoor festivals like the Squamish Valley Music Festival. Alex Vyskocil, originally from Calgary, took over from Hoffman as the new Commodore talent buyer. In addition to continuing to book national and touring music acts, Vyskocil has brought in different kinds of shows, including comedy acts like Adam Carolla in 2012. In what first seemed an unlikely move, he's also broadened the venue's focus to include sports entertainment, hosting several sold-out nights with a western-Canada-based wrestling league, the ECCW, and placing a wrestling ring in the middle of the Commodore dance floor.

Vyskocil admits that the concert business presents him with more difficult margins than his predecessors had to deal with. "Booking the Commodore doesn't get any easier, but you can't put bad shows in there. We're not going to start showing movies there, just to fill it. The Commodore is one of the most iconic music rooms in Canada, but the room allows you to do many things, and we are trying new ones," Vyskocil says. "I like the fact that fans who go to a drag show feel as comfortable going there as the crowd that comes for wrestling or the fan who comes for a hip-hop show." Vyskocil says that some of his favourite shows during his tenure have included Franz Ferdinand, Santigold, Frank Ocean, and the Imagine Dragons,

Wrestling at the Commodore
Ballroom, January 2014.
Photos: Carman Kwan

Above: Die Antwoord, May 22, 2014. Photo: Jamie Taylor Concert Addicts.com

Right: Franz Ferdinand onstage at the Commodore, September 26, 2004. Photo: Kevin Statham

but adds that "anytime a legend comes in to play the room, it's great—k.d. lang and Dwight Yoakam have performed there in the last couple of years. When a legend plays timeless music in a legendary venue, it's great."

In 2011, partly to showcase the history of the room and also to pay tribute to Drew Burns, Commodore general manager Gord Knights instigated a project to document all the shows that have occurred at the Commodore on its website. The author of this book participated in the year-long project, and the website features the exact dates, band by band, night by night, of all the acts that have performed there since the early 1970s when Burns began his era at the Commodore. Through it all, Knights has remained acutely aware of Burns' significance to the room, citing "his years of mentorship and keen business sense, and his personal love for the Commodore. Today," says Knights, "we operate the Ballroom with the same focus. We consider ourselves curators of a very valuable and fragile resource in our cultural community. Drew was our founder. We try to keep things current and make sure that there will be a future at the Commodore—we want our kids and their kids to be able to see shows there and experience what we've experienced, that tangible joy people get from experiencing music so closely. When people get that, it changes their lives, and it certainly changed mine."

In his eighties, Drew Burns continued to enjoy retirement but still kept occasional tabs on what was happening at the old room. Despite the unceremonious end of his tenure at the Commodore, Burns remained characteristically upbeat. "The place holds good memories for me. You know there's no place like it in Canada, and there never will be. It's world-renowned

The record for playing the Commodore more than any other act in recent years goes to 54-40. Since their first appearance in 1982, the Vancouver-based band has performed there more than fifty times. "For our fiftieth show," recalls bassist Brad Merritt, "the Commodore gave every patron a special ticket for a drink at the end of the night so they could toast to us and our fifty shows. That was phenomenal." Photo: Adam PW Smith

Drew Burns outside the Commodore (above) and his spot on the BC Entertainment Hall of Fame Starwalk on Granville Street. Photos: Dan Toulgoet, 2013.

now. There are people in the music business all over the world who know it."

Burns was immortalized in the BC Entertainment Hall of Fame Star Walk on Granville Street. (When Granville's sidewalks were pulled up in the street's major redesign in 2009, however, Burns' star was inexplicably moved by the city from outside the front door of the Commodore to a spot further north, up the street.) Of his own legacy at the Commodore, Burns spoke of it with a mixture of modesty and pride, saying, "There are new people there now, and they are adding to the history of the Commodore. They'll be legends, eventually."

What meant the most to Burns were "the people, from the musicians to the people who went there, who stop to thank me because they remember that I treated them well or because I gave them a start or helped them somehow," he said. And he admitted that, even though he hadn't been involved with the Ballroom since he retired more than fifteen years ago, people still stopped him on the street and asked how things were down at the Commodore. "I always tell them," he said with a smile, "'I haven't seen you there for a while. Why don't you come down sometime and say hi?'"

Sadly, just weeks before this book was published, Drew Burns passed away aged eighty-one.

Down on Granville Street, on a late-summer evening, it's another busy night on the strip, and the sidewalks are crowded. Some people stop to notice the names set into the sidewalks; while these enshrine the city's entertainment legends, in the alleyway behind the Commodore, plenty of music legends have sneaked through the backstage doors over the decades. For all of Vancouver's lauded natural beauty, this alleyway, where the band's buses pull up, is sometimes the only spot in the city that performers see as they come and go. While the lively sounds of Granville Street can be heard around the corner, tonight in the alleyway, veteran stagehand Tim Tilton is alone at the door preparing for the load-out, much as he's done for decades. He looks up at the sky for a moment to see if it's going to rain. The band's bus cruises into the alley and stops in position. Tilton knows the bus driver from previous tours at the Commodore, and they share a joke. A full house inside is enjoying an encore, and the rumble of the music can be heard coming from the second-floor windows.

In front of the club on Granville Street, as the crowds file past the building, Gord Knights has come down to take in the scene. It's been a good night, and he chats for a few moments with the doormen who await the thousand people about to file out of the building when the show ends. A couple walking down the street stop for a moment and get the attention of one of the Ballroom's doormen. They ask him the question that passersby on Granville Street have put to Commodore doormen since the 1930s. "Who's playing tonight?"

Photo: Jamie Taylor, 2014

AFTERWORD & ACKNOWLEDGMENTS

IN SOME WAYS, the original spark for this book struck in 2011 when I was asked by Commodore Ballroom general manager Gord Knights to assist in building an archival record of all its past shows for their new website.

It was a daunting proposal. Aside from the size of the project, the source material was surprisingly vague and incomplete; while certain shows and dates were recalled by those who worked at the Commodore and audiences alike, no official records had been kept over the years, or if they were, the (pre-digital) ledgers and calendars were long lost. The demands of running a live-music venue are naturally more focused on what's happening tomorrow night or coming next week than on looking back at yesterday. And although since 1999, when House of Blues and Live Nation Canada took over the Commodore, a list of more recent concerts has been on file on at the company's offices, they were not conveniently accessible to the public, nor could they be used to showcase the history of the venue.

Creating this list was like building the Great Wall of China out of Lego, and for me it meant countless hours in the following year and a half to alternately take on the roles of historian, musicologist, and detective. I scoured thousands of newspaper and entertainment weekly microfiche scans, old

calendars marked with penciled-in notes, and other documents to put together a day-by-day look at the Commodore over more than forty years. The show archive went public in March 2013 and has remained a popular feature on the site. It is continually updated and in some ways can be considered a companion to this book.

Over the months I spent logging the shows, bands, and concert dates for the archive, a picture emerged of how the Commodore developed at a time when the live music industry itself was growing exponentially. While national and international music trends and tastes were reflected in the music onstage at the ballroom, I could also see what Vancouverites themselves were going to hear and how our tastes could be seen to broaden, as world music acts, which just a few years earlier might have played to an empty house, now filled the ballroom. Unexpectedly, the Commodore emerged, through its archives, as a cultural barometer of the city. Admittedly, it was also just fun to browse through the list, recalling shows I'd seen or played as a musician and read about ones I'd missed.

Indeed, perhaps this book was set into motion in 1990, when as a nineteen-year-old I first began to go to the Commodore. Within two years, I played there myself, and the archive revealed to me that while playing in a number of local bands (chiefly the Real McKenzies, Bocephus King, and the Town Pants), I'd been on that stage more than twenty-five times. I'd like to think I have a few more Commodore shows left in me yet, though perhaps I won't be able to catch up to Spirit of the West, Jim Byrnes, or Blue Rodeo, who now count over forty performances at the Ballroom, or 54-40, who've played more than fifty times. Of course, Ole Olsen

and His Commodores, the house orchestra that performed there regularly throughout the 1940s might have us all beat!

As an audience member and a performer, I thought I already had a deep appreciation of the venue. But in 2006, while still working as a writer and musician, I began to pick up some extra work at the Commodore as one of the production managers at House of Blues concerts, who helped to run shows at the ballroom and other venues. I even began to pick up occasional shifts working as one of the club doormen. I now chalk it all up as "undercover research" for this project because it gave me a much greater understanding of the clockwork of the venue.

In the wake of the 2012 publication of my previous book, *Liquor, Lust, and the Law: The Story of Vancouver's Legendary Penthouse Nightclub*, I bumped into former Commodore manager Drew Burns, who congratulated me on the book's success. When he offhandedly remarked, "You should be the one to do a Commodore book. I don't have time to do one myself," I took it as a positive omen, and it galvanized the decision on what my next book would be about. I never asked Drew if he was just kidding around with me, or if he didn't think I'd actually go ahead with the project, but for better or worse, his remark set into motion the book you now hold in your hands.

Without question, my gratitude goes to Drew Burns. Over lunches, phone calls, and emails, Drew was patient and generous while responding to my countless questions about the Commodore. Every single person I interviewed for the book told me not only how much he was liked, but loved. It's no surprise. As the proprietor of the Commodore for more than twenty-five years, during a crucial period in its history,

Burns did more than any single club owner in the history of Vancouver to alter the landscape of the nightclub and music scene. He played an important role in the culture of Vancouver itself—and looked like he had a lot of fun doing it. He gave so many musicians help when they needed it, if not their start in the business. While he wasn't there when the Commodore opened, many consider him its founder.

I looked forward to presenting Drew with his own copy of this book and personally thanking him. I hoped to hear a few more stories, even if it was too late to fit them into the book. I wanted to see his enjoyment, knowing that readers had learned about his life and contributions to Vancouver's cultural history. But on the eve of this book going to press, Drew passed away at his home in Vancouver. I am left to join the many people who appreciated and had great respect for Drew. Beyond my thanks for his help with this book, I will always be grateful for his love for the Commodore and for being so welcoming—he made an entire city feel welcome there. This book is dedicated to him.

Many individuals and groups made contributions without which this book could not have been undertaken or completed. I must thank Paul Haagenson, Ian Low, Alex Vyskocil, Geoff Robins, and Dave Osborne and everyone at the Vancouver office of Live Nation Concerts Canada. In particular, I thank Erik Hoffman whose early interest and support for the book helped me navigate it through the necessary corporate channels. Live Nation generously provided access to their library of modern concert posters and information about the venue. Additional thanks to Marc Gertner at the LNCC office in Toronto for approving certain legal authorizations.

I have tremendous gratitude to my publisher Arsenal Pulp Press: Brian Lam, Robert Ballantyne, and Cynara Geissler, and especially to editor Susan Safyan and production manager Gerilee McBride who have my profound gratitude for their skills, working under a very tight deadline in the editing and layout of the book. This would not have been possible without their patience and support.

At the Commodore itself, I am grateful to Gord Knights, Byron Lonneberg, and Carita Sword, as well as the many long-time staff members, past and present, including managers, bartenders, and stagehands whom I've pestered with frequent questions about their memories of the place; these helped inform the text. Perhaps most of all, I want to thank long-time Commodore stagehand Tim Tilton, who after decades of working at the ballroom, and as an avid music fan, amassed a personal museum of Commodore memorabilia from set lists, bootlegs, posters, photos, backstage passes, and colourful anecdotes, many of which are published in this book for the first time.

Pops Wilson may have claimed to knew every nail in the place in early 1970s, but today Sean Mawhinney, the Commodore's building manager for the last fifteen years, can make that claim as. As a friend with a shared interest in the history of the venue, our conversations over the years gave me insight into the design of the building and how it has changed.

My thanks to Riley O'Connor, Norman Perry, Gerry Barad, and Bud Wandrei, who put up with my many phone calls and emails about the early years of Perryscope. Much of their pioneering model informs the concert industry today, and the Commodore was a crucible for their early work.

It was my great good fortune to have exceptional help from Rob Frith at Neptoon Records in Vancouver. When the Commodore was being renovated in 1999, many old documents, photographs, posters, handbills, and program, some going back to the 1960s, were discarded in a dumpster in the alleyway behind the Commodore. Garbage pickers and binners found much of this material and offered it to Frith for a few dollars. While some might have passed on it as trash, Frith—though initially unaware of the significance of some of the material, like the photos of the Fifth Day Club—understood the worth of its provenance. Frith stored these documents for another fifteen years and generously shared them with me when he learned I was writing this book. These items, in addition to the astounding Commodore poster collection in his Neptoon Poster Archives, are published here for the first time.

I am indebted to the many photographers who provided images for this book. While many had to dig through years of their own archives, they took on the task with relish. All showed enthusiasm, support, and professionalism. My thanks and appreciation to photographers Rebecca Blissett, Charles Campbell, Bev Davies, Lois Klingbeil, Dee Lippingwell, Carman Kwan, Charles Peterson, Ron Vermuelen, Kevin Statham, Adam PW Smith, Sprout, Jamie Taylor, Milos Tosic, and Dan Toulgoet.

A note of thanks to Rob Edmonds at Evoke Design International in Vancouver who has designed and continues to design so many of the wonderful Commodore concert posters that Vancouver residents see on poster poles and walls about town, many of which are reprinted in this book. I have done all I could to find the artists or designers of the decades' old posters published here, but in many cases those artists are unknown. I hope they will contact me so that, in a future edition, we can acknowledge their work.

My thanks to many in the local media (Global Television, the CBC, CKNW, CKWX, the *Georgia Straight* and the *Vancouver Courier*) who rallied interest in the book; the early publicity helped me put out some fishing lines for stories and anecdotes from British Columbians who wanted to share their memories of the Commodore.

Many thanks to Bruce Allen, Jim Allen, Brian Anderson, Tom Anselmi, John Armstrong, Chris Arnett, Norma Arnett, John Atkin, Jean Bain, Kim Barnatt, Squire Barnes, Scott Beadle, Dr. John Belshaw, Jay Bentley, Jeff Boyne, Gyles Brandreth, Jim Byrnes, Tom Carter, Neko Case, Peter Chapman, Dorian Christie, Jason Coleman, Barry Link and Michael Kissinger at the *Vancouver Courier*, Jim Cuddy, Theota Dancer, Tracey Davis, Stuart Derdeyn at the *Province*, Jesse Donaldson, Vince Ditrich, Karen Estrin and Jessica Quan at the Vancouver Heritage Foundation, Luther Fairbairn, Mac Fairbairn, Jay Ferguson, Danny Filippone, Fiona Forbes, Mel McEwen Fraser, Christine Fraser, Jed Gamble, Lawrence Gogo, Patrick Gourlay, Judge Thomas Gove, Johannes Grames, Ryan Grant, Dave Fortune, Robyn Hanson, Al Harlow, Joey Harris, Tom Harrison, Stan Heisie, Mildred Henderson, Pete Henderson, Heritage Vancouver, Colin James, JJ at Scrape Records, Brent Kane, Simon Kendall, Greg Keillor, Michael Kluckner, Sean Lannon, Grant Lawrence, Robin LeRose, Bud Luxford, Donald Luxton, Scott Lyon, Adrian Mack and Mike Usinger at the Georgia Straight, Mike Newburg, John Mackie at the *Vancouver Sun*, Greg MacDonald, Dan Mangan, Grant McDonagh and Zulu Records, Dave Meszaros, Paul Mercs, Brad

Merritt, Paul Myers, Dennis Mills, Vaughn Palmer, Dan Pelkie, James Petrovich, Keith Porteous, Colin Preston, Diane Purvey, Catherine Rose, Dal and Muriel Richards, Svend Robinson, Lani Russwurm, Rene Solomon, Tim Sommer, Sting, Susan Tabata, Mick Thomas, Sharon Tungate, Adam Todd, everyone at the Vancouver Archives, the Vancouver Police Museum, the Vancouver Public Library Special Collections Historical Photographs Section, , George Thorogood, Rob and Beverly Tyrell, Jason Vanderhill, Mel Warner, Paul Way, Stevie Wilson, Les Wiseman, Will Woods and all at Forbidden Vancouver, and Tom Zillich.

Lastly, thanks to all the bands, promoters, managers, stagehands, bartenders, servers, doormen, staff, and the audiences at the Commodore over the years who've made it what is today. It's a credit to all of these people that the Commodore still exists. The venue is just an empty building without people in it, and so many nightclubs and theatres in Vancouver over the years have disappeared or been demolished.

In 2015, the Commodore will celebrate its eighty-fifth anniversary. And while it has official heritage status in Vancouver, the venue has yet to be designated a National Historic Site. I hope this book might help to correct this omission and perhaps also attract consideration from the Rock and Roll Hall of Fame. I believe that when people in Vancouver and abroad realize how many others have walked up its stairs, danced on its dance floor, or appeared on its stage, they will understand how special the place is, and why the neon sign outside reads, "The Fabulous Commodore Ballroom."

Aaron Chapman

The BC Entertainment Hall of Fame Historic Venues ceremony, Commodore Ballroom. Photo: Courtesy of Danny Filippone and the Penthouse Nightclub

REFERENCES

Andrews, Marke. "Watering Holes That Didn't Run Dry." *Vancouver Sun*, September 24, 1982.

Bouchette, R. D. "Lend Me Your Ears." *Vancouver Sun*, December 5, 1930.

————. "Whoopee in Vancouver." *Vancouver Sun*, March 23, 1931.

Buckner, Dianne. "Small Business Tips from Riley O'Connor, Chair of Ticket Giant Live Nation," CBC News/Business. June 1, 2012. http://www.cbc.ca/news/business/small-business-tips-from-riley-o-connor-chair-of-ticket-giant-live-nation-1.1280586. http://www.cbc.ca/news/business/small-business-tips-from-riley-o-connor-chair-of-ticket-giant-live-nation-1.1280586

Bula, Frances. "Is It Time to Tame Granville Street?" *Vancouver Magazine*, April 1, 2013.

"Commodore Ballroom & Beefheart: Never Too Violent." *Georgia Straight,* March 8, 1973.

"Commodore Cabaret Re-opens." *Vancouver Sun*, May 22, 1931.

"The Commodore to Open Tonight." *Vancouver Sun*, December 3, 1930.

"City Police Officer Dies at Fete." *Vancouver Sun*, July 2, 1955.

"Commodore Fans Get Chance to Buy Chunks of History." *Georgia Straight*, January 18, 1996.

Davis, Chuck. ed. *The Vancouver Book*. Vancouver: Evergreen Press, 1976.

————. *The Greater Vancouver Book: An Urban Encyclopedia*. Surrey, BC: Linkman Press, 1997.

————. *The History of Metropolitan Vancouver*. Madeira Park, BC: Harbour Publishing, 2011.

Down, Audrey. "Leisure Goes to a Party." *Vancouver Sun*, June 13, 1969.

Gold, Kerry. "Old Commodore Reincarnated." *Vancouver Sun*, October 6, 1999.

Hall, Neal. "Commodore: 55 Years of Good Times." *Vancouver Sun*, December 1, 1984.

Harrison, Tom. "Gabba Gabba hey … We're da Ramones." *Georgia Straight*, August 11, 1977.

————. "The Most Important Band in Rock and Roll." *Georgia Straight*, January 26, 1979.

————. "Clash Interview: What is Joe Strummer Doing in Biminis?" *Georgia Straight*, February 2, 1979.

"End of an Era with Pump's Passing." *The Province*, July 13, 1997.

Huey, George. "Hagar Opens Concert Series." *The Ubyssey*, January 27, 1978, 17.

"Inspecting New Trainer Plane." *Vancouver Sun*, July 13, 1940.

Kendall, Kay. "21 Steps Lead to Nostalgia." *Vancouver Sun*, October 12, 1973.

Kenney, Mart. *Mart Kenney and His Western Gentlemen*. Saskatoon, SK: Modern Press, 1981.

Keiran, Brian. "Commodore Man: Brian Keiran Talks to Drew Burns." *The Province*, July 19, 1987.

Kluckner, Michael. *Vancouver: The Way It Was*. North Vancouver: Whitecap Books, 1984.

Lecich, John. "The Ballroom's Modest Prince," *Georgia Straight*, July 11–18, 1996, 15–16.

Lee, Bonita. "Virgin Hunting in the Concrete Jungle." *The Ubyssey*, October 18, 1968.

"Let's All Celebrate." *Vancouver Sun*, December 3, 1930.

Luxton, Donald, ed. *Building the West*. Vancouver: Talonbooks, 2007.

Goldberg, Michael. "Devo: Sixties Idealists or Nazis and Clowns?" *Rolling Stone*, December 10, 1981.

Macdonald, Bruce. *Vancouver: A Visual History*. Vancouver: Talonbooks, 1993.

MacGillivray, Alex. "Fifth Day Club." *Vancouver Sun*, September 15, 1967.

Mackie, John. "Ballroom Actually Opened 74 Years Ago." *Vancouver Sun*, December 4, 2004.

———. "Commodore, Tires Horsehair Gave Floor Bounce," *Vancouver Sun*, December 4, 2004.

———. "Dolls Bring Their Glam And Grit Preview." *Vancouver Sun*, February 29, 2008.

———. "Vancouver's Lost Landmarks." *Vancouver Sun*, April 7, 2011.

Mason, Bruce. "Memories Are Great But the Best Is Yet to Come," *The Province*, November 30, 1989.

McDonald, Verne. "Strummer Leads a Pogue-o Party." *Georgia Straight*, October 11, 1991.

McHugh, Duncan. "Bouncing Back." *The Ubyssey* 81, no. 21 (1999): 1–2.

Monk, Katherine. "Last Dance?" *Vancouver Sun*, June 29, 1996.

———. "Commodore Ballroom Fate Now in Hands of High Court." *Vancouver Sun*, June 26, 1996.

———. "Commodore Decision Today." *Vancouver Sun*, June 27, 1996.

———. "Last Waltz Is Sunday as 66-Year-Old Nightspot Closes." *Vancouver Sun*, June 28, 1996.

"New Club De Luxe Has Brilliant Opening." *Vancouver Sun*, December 4, 1930.

"Nick Kogos Made $110,000 Settlement With Income Tax Department." *Vancouver Sun*, February 15, 1951.

Palmer, Vaughn. "Save the Last Dance for Me: The Commodore Turns 50." *Vancouver Sun*, November 30, 1979.

———. "Blondie Wows 'Em." *The Vancouver Express*, January 5, 1979.

———. "Are These Not Men? Close—They Are Devo," *The Vancouver Express*, January 15, 1979

Potter, Greg. "Commodore Celebrates 75 Years of Live Music." *Georgia Straight*, December 2, 2004. http://www.straight.com/commodore-celebrates-75-years-live-music.

Potter, Greg, and Red Robinson. *Backstage Vancouver: A Century of Entertainment Legends*. Madeira Park, BC: Harbour Publishing, 2004.

Raugust, Paul. "Vancouver Goes Boom in the Night." *The Province*, March 13, 1974.

Read, Jeani. "Dolls Sang Trash, That About Says It," *The Province*, March 14, 1974.

Richards, Dal and Jim Taylor. *One More Time!: The Dal Richards Story.* Madeira Park, BC: Harbour Publishing, 2009.

"Safecrackers Raid Commodore Cabaret; Escape with $650." *Vancouver Sun*, July 15, 1940.

"Saturday Night at the Commodore." *Vancouver Sun*, April 4, 1932.

Schneider, Stephen. *Iced: The Story of Organized Crime in Canada.* Mississauga, ON: Wiley, 1993.

Smith, Charlie. "Battle for Ballroom Drags On." *Georgia Straight,* July 4, 1996.

Stanley, Don. "When You're All Trash, Darling, You've Got Image." *Vancouver Sun*, March 14, 1974.

"Three Named in Arson Charge." *Vancouver Daily World*, August 15, 1921.

"Vancouver's Latest Attraction the Commodore Cabaret." *Vancouver Sun*, October 2, 1930.

Wasserman, Jack. "The Town around Us." *Vancouver Sun*, August 17, 1961.

Watson, Dave. "Denizens Remember the Great Times and Bum's Rushes." *Georgia Straight*, July 11, 1996.

"Yeggs Get into Office by Light Well," *Vancouver Sun*, July 15, 1950.

Zillich, Tom. "Swan Songs Set for Commodore." *Kitsilano News*, July 3, 1996.

Television

Gyles Brandreth, "The Lambeth Walk," *The One Show.* BBC TV, February 7, 2013.

Unpublished Documents

Commodore Cabaret Ltd. v Pensionfund Properties Ltd., [1996] 3024. BC Supreme Court, 1996-06-27. C962642. Vancouver Registry.

Greater Vancouver, BC, volume II, City of Vancouver [surveyed] October 1928 by the British Columbia Insurance Underwriters Association, 1928. CVA MAP 599. Located in City of Vancouver Archives.

McInnes, Emily. "70 Years of the Commodore Ballroom 1929–1999." Report prepared for Panther Management, 1999.

"34th Annual Women's Auxiliary to the Health Centre for Children, October 22, 1954." AM1519- PAM 1954-128, item 1954. Located in City of Vancouver Archives.

Interviews

Adams, Bryan. Email interview with author, May 27, 2014.

Allen, Bruce. Interview with author, June 6, 2014.

Anderson, Brian. Telephone interview with author, June 5, 2014.

Armstrong, John. Telephone interview with author, February 7, 2014

Arnett, Norma. Telephone interview with author, March 6, 2014.

Anselmi, Tom. Telephone interview with author, July 8, 2014.

Bain, Jean. Telephone interview with author, March 6, 2014.

Barad, Gerry. Telephone interviews with author, March 27, 2014 and June 30, 2014.

Biafra, Jello. Email interview with author, May 16, 2014.

Boyne, Jeff. Interview with author, June 5, 2014.

Burns, Drew. Interviews with author, Vancouver, BC, May 12, 2012 and April 18, 2013.

Byrnes, Jim. Telephone interview with author, March 12, 2014.

Christie, Dorian. Interview with author, West Vancouver, BC, May 14, 2014.

Cuddy, Jim. Telephone interview with author, March 12, 2014.

Cuthbert, Doug. Telephone interview with author, May 6, 2014.

Derdeyn, Stuart. Telephone interview with author, July 9, 2014.

Fairbairn, Luther. Telephone interview with author, March 11, 2014.

Fortune, Dave. Interview with author, Vancouver, BC, February 14, 2014.

Ferguson, Jay. Telephone interview with author, July 8, 2014.

Gourlay, Patrick. Telephone interview with author, May 14, 2014.

Grant, Jason. Telephone interview with author, May 29, 2014.

Hanson, Robyn. Telephone interview with author, February 14, 2014.

Henderson, Mildred. Interview with author, Burnaby, BC, February 19, 2014.

Hoffman, Erik. Interview with author, Vancouver, BC, April 29, 2014.

James, Colin. Interview with author, North Vancouver, BC, May 7, 2014.

Jeunesse, John. Interview with author, Vancouver, BC, March 19, 2014.

Kane, Brent. Telephone interview with author, March 24, 2014.

Kendall, Simon. Telephone interview with author, May 16, 2014.

Kluckner, Michael. Telephone interview with author, February 11, 2014.

Knights, Gord. Interview with author, Vancouver, BC, June 6, 2014.

Luxford, Bud. Interview with author, Vancouver, BC, April 3, 2014.

MacFarlane, Terry. Telephone interview with author, March 11, 2014.

McDonagh, Grant. Telephone interview with author, May 9, 2014.

Mills, Dennis. Interview with author, Vancouver BC, July 21, 2013.

Mercs, Paul. Interview with author, May 20, 2013.

Merrit, Brad. Telephone interview with author, July 7, 2014.

Myers, Paul. Telephone interview, February 19, 2014.

O'Connor, Riley. Telephone interview, March 27, 2014.

Palmer, Vaughn. Telephone interview with author, March 27, 2014.

Perry, Norman. Telephone interview with author, June 9, 2014.

Richards, Dal. Interview with author, Vancouver, BC, February 22, 2013.

Sommer, Tim. Telephone interview with author, June 5, 2014.

Sting. Interview with author, Vancouver, BC, February 20, 2014.

Tyrell, Robert. Telephone interview with author, March 7, 2014.

Usinger, Mike. Interview with author, Vancouver, BC, July 9, 2014.

Vyskocil, Alex. Telephone interview with author, July 10, 2014.

Wandrei, Bud. Interview with author, Vancouver, BC, March 13, 2014.

INDEX

Photo: Rebecca Blissett

AARON CHAPMAN

AARON CHAPMAN is a writer, historian, and musician. Born and raised in Vancouver, he has been a contributor to the *Vancouver Courier*, the *Georgia Straight,* and CBC radio. His 2012 book *Liquor, Lust, and The Law: The Story of Vancouver's Legendary Penthouse Nightclub*, published by Arsenal Pulp Press, was a BC bestseller and a finalist for the BC Book Prize (Roderick Haig-Brown Regional Prize). His work is also featured in the anthology *Vancouver Confidential* (Anvil Press, 2014), edited by John Belshaw. A graduate of the University of British Columbia, he is a member of Heritage Vancouver and the Point Roberts Historical Society. *aaronchapman.net*